GREG CHAPPELL

Greg Chappell is one of Australia's greatest international sporting stars. He has sometimes been described as the finest batsman Australia has produced since Don Bradman. He led the Australian cricket team to many memorable victories during his Test career. Appointed an MBE for his services to cricket, he was a member of the Australian Cricket Board from 1984 until he resigned in 1988.

After a career in the finance industry, Greg became the managing director of Fundamental Golf and Leisure Ltd in 1993. He has also been a regular television sports commentator and has produced a number of cricket books. He was the subject of Adrian McGregor's biography, *Greg Chappell*. Greg is currently coaching the South Australian cricket team.

GREG CHAPPELL'S
HEALTH AND FITNESS
REPAIR MANUAL

Always consult your doctor before beginning a diet or exercise program.

A Hodder & Stoughton Book
First published in 1998 by
Hodder Headline Australia Pty Limited
(A member of the Hodder Headline Group)
10–16 South Street, Rydalmere NSW 2116

Reprinted 1998 (twice)

Published in association with
Brewster Publishers Pty Ltd
PO Box 3231, Tamarama NSW 2026

National Library of Australia Cataloguing-in-Publication data:

Chappell, Greg, 1948–.
Greg Chappell's health and fitness repair manual.

ISBN 0 7336 0961 9.

1. Men - Health and hygiene - Australia. 2. Physical fitness for men - Australia. I. Title. II. Title : Health and fitness repair manual.

613.04230994

Printed in Australia by Griffin Press, Adelaide

Contents

INTRODUCTION

THIS BOOK IS intended for a special group of people: middle-aged men. It is a group I belong to myself. I turned forty as far back as 1988 and fifty just as this book was going to press, so I have had plenty of time to analyse the subject of middle age first-hand. The most important thing I have discovered about middle age is that it can be an immensely interesting and satisfying period in a man's life. It is a time when most of us have achieved some degree of stability in our affairs. This isn't to say we have reached a dead end. For me personally, the opposite has been true. Since turning forty my life has taken more new, challenging directions than it ever did before. But in middle age we are free of many previous pressures—pressures of career-building, of home-buying, of family-raising. We are in a position to enjoy the present rather than be stressing ourselves about the future.

There is a catch, though. Middle age also happens to be a period when most men begin to experience an accelerating physical decline. They start to see and feel the symptoms of aging in a hundred different ways. They develop health problems and become less mobile. For a sizeable proportion of Australian men these twin afflictions—illness and loss of mobility—are the ruination of middle age. I am hardly breaking news by saying this. Everyone knows it to be true. The amazing thing is that so many men do nothing about it. The reason, I believe, is that they do not know what to do.

That is what this book is about—doing something to stop the slide.

CHAPTER ONE
FORTY SOMETHING

> ***One of the most important things I have discovered about middle age is that it can be an immensely interesting and satisfying period in a man's life.***

WHEN WE ENTER MIDDLE AGE we are at one of life's most important crossroads. We can allow our body to continue its middle-age decline, growing fatter and slower, suffering more and more illnesses, and becoming less and less active as our bodies start to seize up; or we can arrest the process by a bold intervention. By changing certain areas of our lifestyle, we can make ourselves fitter and healthier, and by doing this we can ensure not only that we stay active throughout our middle age but that we prolong this active middle age far beyond the normal span.

Happily, there is a secret to doing this. It is this: the state of your health depends primarily on what you eat. It is a simple concept, but it is actually a fundamental truth of life which I have come to believe in fervently. What you put in your mouth largely determines how rapidly you age, how energetic you feel, how sick you are, how fat you grow and how soon you

... by changing certain areas of our lifestyle, we can make ourselves fitter and healthier ...

die. The corollary of this is that by adopting new eating habits and by committing yourself to regular exercise you can transform yourself physically and, perhaps, change your mental outlook, too. I know this to be true because I have done it myself.

So this is primarily a book about nutrition. If you did not know it already, you will know before many more pages that I have become a pure vegetarian. The reason I am a vegetarian is simply that I am convinced it is the healthiest way to eat and that it gives me my best chance of enjoying a long, active and illness-free middle age. The purpose of this book, though, is not to persuade you to become a vegetarian. I am not looking for converts. I am realistic enough to recognise that few people can bring themselves to give up meat entirely. I accept this, but I also believe that if you are an ordinary, meat-eating Australian male the most important, the most beneficial thing you can do for your health is reduce your intake of animal protein; that is, meat and dairy products. Unlike most other things we try to give up for the sake of our health, meat is actually not hard to do without.

GIVE YOUR LIFE A LIFT

Good health is not the only reward you gain from becoming healthy. By this I mean that the process of becoming healthy can have an uplifting effect on your life in general. You will feel better about yourself. You will be free of the guilt you have probably felt for ignoring your health. You will also have an interest in life you did not have before—and do not doubt that the pursuit of good health can become an absorbing interest. If the subject of health really grabs you as it has me, it will influence everything you do.

> One of the rewards of becoming pro-active in attaining good health is the knowledge you are reducing the chance of contracting some life-shortening illness like heart disease or cancer. Striving for good health does not guarantee you will avoid cancer or some other illness, but at least you will no longer feel like a sitting duck waiting for the illness to strike.

Making an effort to improve your health and fitness also has what some people call an 'empowering' effect. Just knowing you are in good health and good physical shape boosts your morale and self-esteem. What you are really experiencing is a sense of freedom—freedom from all the limitations imposed on you by being unfit, overweight, stiff-jointed or prematurely feeble.

In other words, you have the satisfaction of knowing that in any situation that arises you will be able to choose from all the options available. Many middle-aged men no longer have a choice of options. If they are invited to a tennis afternoon at a friend's house, they have to decline, knowing they are no longer mobile enough to get around the court. Or if their car breaks down on some remote bush road, they do

Making an effort to improve your health and fitness also has what some people call an 'empowering' effect.

not have the option of walking to the petrol station they passed ten kilometres back. They have to sit in the car hoping some other vehicle goes by the in the next few hours. If this seems far-fetched, ask yourself the question: would I be capable of walking the ten kilometres?

Some people will be surprised that a former cricketer is writing this kind of book. After all, cricketers do not have a reputation for being fussy about what they eat. The British soccer coach Tommy Docherty once said: 'Cricket is organised loafing. It's the only sport you can put on weight playing.' Unfortunately this is true. You do see plenty of overweight cricketers, even at the elite level of the game. Some of them eat second-rate food yet expect to perform as first-rate international sportsmen. I think they are foolish and irresponsible, but I find it hard to condemn them, for we were no better in our day. We ate second-rate food, too.

I might still be eating second-rate food if circumstances had not placed me in a situation where I was forced to think hard about all aspects of my health. Not all men are so lucky. They breeze along, eating whatever they have a taste for and doing little in the way of physical exercise. It isn't that they do not know about the 'ravages of middle age' which lie ahead. It's just that they close their minds to it. Or if they do think about it, they accept it as inevitable.

But it is not inevitable. It is within the power of each of us to reshape our lives for thirty or forty years ahead by deciding today to change the way we eat and to start exercising. It is not hard to do. All you need is the will. Your body will do the rest.

CHAPTER TWO
THE WAY TO GOOD HEALTH: A THREE-POINT PLAN

Some people think a balanced diet means a bag of hot chips in each hand.

MANY HUNDREDS of books have been written over the past twenty years about good health and how to achieve it. If you sat down and read them all you would be none the wiser, because each tells a different story. The science of health is still largely a collection of theories, and theories have a habit of contradicting each other.

This book is not based on theory. It is based on my personal experience. Up until I was thirty my lifestyle was the same as any other Australian's. I 'lived well', as the saying goes, eating meat-based and dairy-rich food in the same large quantities most other Australians eat them. In fact, I 'lived better' than most. As an international cricketer, I was on the road for a large proportion of each year, staying in hotels and eating room-service meals, restaurant meals and junk food.

Of course I was not living well at all. I was living badly, although I was not even remotely conscious of this at the time. The very word 'nutrition' seemed foreign to me. Nutrition was something health nuts might get excited about, but it was not something a normal, red-blooded Australian needed to be interested in.

At about the age of thirty the thought at last dawned on me that the way I was eating might be affecting my health. Looking back on it, I suppose it was a type of awakening, because from then on I steadily became more and more interested in the subject of health, in particular the connection between health and nutrition. Since then I have studied the subject from every angle, and by trial and error have moved steadily closer to what I am convinced is the way to achieve maximum health, especially if you are middle-aged. It has definitely worked for me, and unless your body's basic physiology is somehow different from mine, which is highly unlikely, it ought to work for you, too.

What I have found may be presented as a three-point plan. The first two are essential and the third, extremely advisable.

The three points are:

- ***Eat nutritious food***

This is really the key to it all. It means not only eating more good food (vegetables, fruit and complex carbohydrates such as bread and pasta) but also less bad food. At the top of the list of bad foods are dairy products. Generally, you need to cut your consumption of animal protein to a minimum. In fact, the closer you come to a vegetarian style of eating, the better your chance of achieving optimum health.

cholesterol that are found in animal protein.

It is a common experience for middle-aged people who have cut down on meat and dairy products to find they no longer suffer from the indigestion that may well have been afflicting them for years in one of its various forms. There is a simple explanation for this. Animal products tend to acidify the system. By reducing the intake of animal products, you reduce the acidity, which in turn results in a disappearance of indigestion. The fact is that all foods except raw fruits and vegetables are acid-forming, but animal protein is the most acid-forming.

Calcium

Many people wanting to strengthen their bones eat and drink dairy products deliberately, believing they are a rich source of calcium. They may be *rich* in calcium, yet to rely on them as a *source* of calcium may be a very wrong move. There is any amount of research to show that dairy products can have exactly the opposite effect. The reasoning is that proteins in milk and cheese acidify the system, disrupting the body's pH balance. The body will go to any lengths to restore the pH balance, and the way it does this is by leaching alkaline minerals, most notably calcium, out of the bones. So instead of strengthening the bones, the dairy products can actually weaken them.

No matter how great your intake of calcium may be, if your diet is high in protein you will be in a negative calcium balance. Eskimos provide an interesting case study here. They have a high intake of calcium from fish bones, but they also have a high intake of animal protein from fish. The result is they have the highest rate of osteoporosis in the world.

Various studies have also pointed to the fact that the ratio of calcium to phosphorus is very important. In Western societies the intake of phosphorus is generally double what it should be. High levels of phosphorus are found in red meat (typically one part calcium to fifteen parts phosphorus); processed canned meats; processed cheeses and cottage cheese; soft drinks (phosphoric acid is usually added to protect tooth enamel); breads, cereals and grain products; instant soups and puddings; and baked products (phosphate is a common additive in baking powder). When the body wants to eliminate excess phosphorus, it uses calcium to do it, thus leaching calcium from the body via the urine. The more animal protein, especially red meat, consumed, the greater the loss of calcium from the bones.

THE IDEAL DIET: A BREAKDOWN

It is hard to be too specific about what an ideal diet should consist of, given that each of us is different from everyone else, but broad guidelines are certainly available. Here is a recommended breakdown by quantity (weight, not volume) of the kinds of food we should eat each day to achieve optimum health: fresh fruit and vegetables 75 per cent; starchy foods (bread, potatoes, pumpkin, rice) 10 per cent; protein-rich foods (meat, cheese, eggs, nuts, legumes) 7.5 per cent; sugar-rich foods (sugar, honey, dried fruits) 5 per cent; fat-rich foods (oil, margarine, butter, cream) 2.5 per cent at the most.

This is the kind of breakdown that we all, both meat-eaters and vegetarians, should aim for. Vegetarians would eliminate the animal foods, of course, yet as a general rule the proportions for the different categories of food hold true. It will be seen that fresh fruit and vegetables should comprise about three-quarters of your diet if you wish to eat as healthily as possible. This leads to a further question: what fruit and vegetables, specifically, should you eat and in which proportion? The short answer is that it does not really matter. Provided you eat a reasonable range of them you need not worry too much about which type. Variety is the key. For instance, if apples and bananas are the only fruit you eat, then your range of fruit is deficient.

IRON RICH

Here are a few other points to keep in mind. If you are switching to a pure or mainly vegetarian style of eating, you will need to include iron-rich plant foods in your diet. This isn't difficult.

Green leafy vegetables are a good source of iron, and of these raw spinach is about the best. Broccoli and cabbage are excellent, and cucumber, cauliflower, lettuce and beet tops are good, too. Spinach in its cooked form is not so good, the reason being that when cooked it produces an acid which can inhibit the absorption of nutrients. Fruit is another good source of iron. Here, in order, are some of the best in this regard: strawberries, apricots, lemons, blueberries and pineapple.

Also, try to include a number of orange-coloured fruits and vegetables (citrus fruits, carrots, sweet potatoes, mangoes) in your diet, because these contain betacarotene, which is converted to vitamin A in the body. As for vitamin C —well, most fruits and vegetables, especially in their raw form, contain this important vitamin in some degree. Citrus fruits and juices, blackcurrants, broccoli and brussels sprouts are particularly good sources.

Actually, the question of which fruits and vegetables you eat is not so important as how you eat them.

The rule here is to eat fruit and vegetables as often as possible in the raw (uncooked) state.

Samantha Backman, a Coffs Harbour nutrition consultant whose work I admire, has strong views on this subject, which are based on the fact that raw fruit and vegetables are the only alkali-producing foods available to us. All other foods are acid-producing—and animal protein is the most acid-producing of all.

The point she makes is that our bodies are best able to maintain a correct pH balance if 80 per cent of our diet consists of alkali-producing foods and 20 per cent acid-producing. In the modern Western diet, though, the proportions are the other way around—80 per cent acid and 20 per cent alkali—which is the root cause of many health complaints, osteoporosis being just one of them.

Nutrition is not everything, but it is almost everything

There are other reasons for eating raw fruit and vegetables. They are obviously our best source of nutrients, given that many nutrients are damaged or destroyed by the cooking process. Raw fruit and vegetables also provide the body with essential enzymes which the body otherwise has to manufacture itself at considerable cost. Now I realise most people would find it hard to switch suddenly to a diet consisting mainly of raw fruit and vegetables, but it is nevertheless the goal to aim for. Backman has found in her work that the people who do switch to this kind of diet rarely wish to switch back after they experience the health benefits. As she says, they soon come to regard any food that has been cooked as 'dead' food.

Nutrition is not everything, but it is almost everything. There are things affecting our health which we cannot control: the quality of the air, the state of the weather, the danger of infection. There is one thing, though, over which we have complete control: the food we put in our mouths. Where our health is concerned, this is the most important influence of all.

CHAPTER THREE
Early days

I grew up in the kind of meat-eating family that was the norm in Australia in the 1950s and 1960s.

LOOKING BACK, THE odd thought strikes me that if I had been healthier at the time I played cricket for Australia I might never have bothered delving into the subject of health. As it was, I was plagued by minor ailments throughout my twenties. This puzzled me at the time. It was hard to understand why someone as young, fit and athletic as me should be so afflicted. It was because of this that I felt driven to do something about the problem myself, instead of simply taking the pills that the doctors prescribed for me. The reason for the ailments, it later emerged, was simple, and it all had to do with what I ate and drank.

Let me say something about my eating habits then. I grew up in the kind of meat-eating family that was the norm in Australia in the 1950s and 1960s. Meat was the basis of almost every meal, starting with bacon and eggs in the morning, which meant we ate large quantities of fried, fatty foods: steaks, casseroles, sausages, chops, roasts. My father's tastes in meat were more extreme than ours. He had a liking for things like tripe and brains, neither of which I could ever face up to.

I am sure I would have played better cricket if I had eaten better. I would certainly have had more energy.

If anything, my eating habits got worse after I began playing top-level cricket. I rarely ate much breakfast, so by the time I arrived at the cricket ground in the morning I felt hungry. There were always plates of sandwiches available in the dressing-room, and from as early as 10 a.m. I would start to fill up on these. I used to 'graze' on sandwiches for the whole of the day (unless, of course, I was out in the middle fielding), which caused my team-mates to wonder how someone so long and lean managed to put so much food away. At lunch, whether or not I was batting, fielding or just sitting in the dressing-room, I would eat whatever was on the table, usually a heavy, meat-based meal which would have been hard to digest. Cakes and biscuits followed at the tea break.

It was much the same when I played in England. I have awful memories of the stodgy lunches, mostly variations of meat plus potatoes, that were served when I played a couple of seasons of county cricket there. Nobody who has eaten in a cricket pavilion in England could forget the potatoes. There were old potatoes, new potatoes, boiled potatoes, baked potatoes, fried potatoes and, most commonly of all, mashed potatoes. Stews were common and were a personal favourite of mine, not because they were particularly tasty but because they were easy to wolf down. As far as I was concerned, the less time spent on eating at the table the better.

So my diet as a cricketer was far from healthy. Knowing what I know now, I am sure I would have played better cricket if I had eaten better. I would certainly have had more energy. The fact is, it takes energy to digest food. Eat a heavy meal at lunch and you can count on feeling sluggish in the afternoon. I experienced this as a cricketer, but at the time I did not understand why. It was most noticeable when I was sitting in the dressing-room, waiting to bat or having batted. I used to feel a lethargy come over me in the middle of the afternoon. Sometimes I found myself nodding off to sleep. This would have been bad enough at any time, but it was a real worry if I was padded up, waiting to bat. At these times I used to go to the back of the dressing-room and jump up and down to try to shake myself into a state of alertness.

THE MILK PROBLEM

Then there was the milk problem. This, too, had early origins. At primary school I was always one of the shortest in the class. I was also one of the skinniest. I was self-conscious about this and spent my formative years trying to put on weight. I wanted to look brawnier, and the simplest way to do this, I decided, was to drink milk. So I drank milkshakes whenever I could, and I also drank milk from the fridge by the litre. In my teenage years I must have downed well over five litres of milk a week on average. Food was of little interest to me. It was something I had to have to stay alive, of course, but for the most part I looked upon meals as a nuisance. Meals interfered with playing sport. When it came to a choice between skipping a meal or missing out on a game of cricket, baseball or football, I always skipped the meal.

The milk-drinking habit stuck with me even after I started playing

When it came to a choice between skipping a meal or missing out on a game of cricket, baseball or football, I always skipped the meal.

first-class cricket. Most cricketers, myself included, had little or no understanding of nutrition. We tended to eat badly or not at all. This was especially so once the season had got under way and the team was on the road, travelling from State to State and staying in hotels. Although I did not realise it at the time, this affected my health. By the middle of the season I would start to feel run down. Unfortunately for me, I also developed throat problems of one kind or another.

My tonsils were at the centre of it all. As a child I suffered repeatedly from tonsillitis, ear infections and various other health problems associated with the tonsils. My brother Ian, five years older than me, had his tonsils out in the early 1950s, when doctors used to remove them as a matter of course. By the time I was old enough to have my tonsils taken out, doctors were shying away from doing the operation, so I had to live with my problem tonsils. In fact, I lived with them until 1975, just before the tour of England that year, when at last we parted company in St Andrew's Hospital in Brisbane.

The standard response to my various throat infections was to see a doctor and get a prescription for some strong antibiotics. None of the doctors I saw seemed too interested in discovering the underlying cause of the problem. I wasn't too interested either. My one concern was to get rid of the sore throat, or whatever else was ailing me, as quickly as possible so I could keep playing and not miss a game. In this way I gradually fell into an unfortunate cycle. Sore throats, doctors, antibiotics—they followed each other in an endless sequence every summer.

None of these health complaints was too serious, but the fact that one followed another ought to have made me wonder much earlier if there was something fundamentally wrong with my health. The trouble had first shown up as far back as 1968 when I played my first season of English county cricket for Somerset. I did not feel completely well while I was over there, but it was only after I came back to Australia and underwent a medical check before starting work as an insurance salesman with the AMP Society that it was discovered I had had glandular fever.

I had only just turned twenty, so I should have rebounded from an illness like this in no time; in fact, that bout of glandular fever seemed to affect me for years. I continued to suffer from the sore throats. On each occasion, the antibiotics the doctors gave me cleared up the problem. But the relief was never more than temporary. For most of the 1970s, the period when I was at my peak as a cricketer, I went from one sore throat to the next, from one course of antibiotics to the next.

It was a chiropractor, not a doctor, who eventually helped me break the cycle. I went to him for treatment for a neck problem, a legacy of an old baseball injury, which was causing me problems whenever I batted or fielded in slips for any length of time. The chiropractor asked me about my general health, and I told him about the sore throats and other complaints. He said he suspected there was some root cause and raised the possibility that my diet was to blame. This was the first time anyone had suggested such a thing, so I listened closely. He asked for the details of my diet. I told him about the hotel meals, the fast food, the cheese sandwiches in the dressing-room, the heavy lunches in the pavilion, the milkshakes.

All this convinced him that my eating habits were the source of the problems. He gave me some literature on the pros and cons of eating red meat and consuming dairy products. Included in it, I remember, was a report of a recent comparative study of elite athletes in the United States, whose fitness had been found to improve sharply when they gave up dairy products. There was also some information about the health consequences of eating red meat and about the allergic effects of dairy products. It was all general information, but when I read it I felt it had been written especially for me. The health problems described in it were my health problems. I was not entirely convinced, but I decided there and then to try abstaining from red meat and dairy products for the time being and see if I felt any better.

I wanted to extend early middle age—that is, the active period we generally associate with the forties—for another thirty or forty years.

That was in 1979. Since that day I have not knowingly touched milk, cheese or any other form of dairy product. There were several times in the next few years when I ate red meat, simply because it was put in front of me at a barbecue or some other social occasion, or as an ingredient of a pasta dish, for example. By and large, though, I gave up red meat at that time, too.

The experiment proved an immediate success. Within days of giving up dairy products and red meat my health seemed to improve. To some extent this may have been because I had conditioned myself mentally to feel better, but there was concrete evidence too. For as long as I could remember I'd had a post-nasal drip. I'd had it for so many years that I had long since ceased to be conscious of it. Suddenly, to my complete surprise, my nasal passages and the back of my throat dried up.

New sense of wellbeing

The new sense of wellbeing I experienced was extraordinary. I felt fitter and had more energy. For the first time in my cricket career I found myself actually enjoying the regular fitness training—running laps of the oval, and so on—which had always been a hard grind. I could feel the training doing me good instead of just making me tired. With hindsight, there is no doubt that the reason for the sudden improvement was that I was no longer contaminating my system with dairy products. It has been suggested that as many as 90 per cent of the population are allergic to dairy foods. In most cases, the symptoms are negligible and people ignore them. If I had not been subjected to the physical strain of playing top-level sport for much of the year, I might have been able to ignore them, too.

The fact that I could feel so much better simply by amending my diet opened my eyes showed me what a big bearing nutrition can have on how healthy we are. I find it astonishing to recall that this idea was then new to me. None of the doctors who'd treated me had ever spelled it out in those terms, perhaps because they themselves were blissfully unaware of it. I had not read it in any newspaper or magazine. Yet it ought to be the first rule of good health. It cannot be over-stressed and it cannot be repeated too many times: by and large the state of your health depends on what you eat and drink.

AN ABIDING INTEREST

So by the early 1980s I had come to view the whole subject of health through very different eyes. I was actively searching out information about nutrition, because I was now coming to realise that this was the key to everything. My wife, Judy, shared the new interest in nutrition, and we naturally became much more conscious of the kind of food we were providing to our three children. Dairy foods were soon phased out of our children's diets with what I believe were beneficial results.

For fourteen years, from 1979 to 1993, I read everything about nutrition I could lay my hands on and I talked about it to anyone I came upon who seemed to have a knowledge of the subject. I also experimented with various types of food to find out, by trial and error, which of them suited me best and which were best for me. Gradually I came to form my own views on the subject, views I had collected here and there from all manner of sources and which, in many cases, I had reshaped in the light of my own experience.

Many of the books, papers and articles I read were written by people who had suffered some health problem of their own (usually heart disease or cancer) or been close to someone who had. In most cases they had become disillusioned by the way mainstream medicine had tried to deal with the problem and had set out to find a health solution of their own. What impressed me was that nearly all these people had come, quite independently, to basically the same conclusion: they had decided that nutrition, not drugs, was the key.

The more I read, the more I became convinced that this was true. So I set out to improve my health by improving my diet. My aim was not to try to live to a great age. Rather, it was to make the most of middle age. I wanted to be fit enough and healthy enough to lead a vigorous life for as long as I could. I wanted to extend early middle age—that is, the active period we generally associate with the forties—for another thirty or forty years. In my own mind I had a personal goal to aim for. I wanted not merely to be able to play golf at eighty but to be able to walk around the course when I did it.

CHAPTER FOUR
MIDDLE AGE

Science tells us that human cells are capable of living between 120 and 140 years, so there is no excuse for being old at sixty or sixty-five.

MIDDLE AGE SEEMS to take an unusually heavy toll on former sportsmen. We have all seen former footballers who are bandy-legged, walk with a limp and have gnarled knuckles and hands. Former cricketers tend to have bad backs, stiff joints and skin conditions, not to mention the many other complaints that middle-aged men are prone to. In my own playing days I used to see many former cricketers at the grounds, and I was struck by the fact that, for their age, they were not on the whole great physical specimens. They had poor posture and did not move about easily. At the time, it occurred to me that if I was going to end up like them I did not have a great future to look forward to.

It wasn't until I took an interest in nutrition that I realised I did not have to end up like that—that it was within my power to prevent it. I realised that by controlling what I ate and how I lived I could take some control over the aging process.

There is no doubt that the onset of middle age makes people think of their mortality. This isn't to say they start worrying about dying, for most of them have every hope of living for a long time yet. But by the time we reach our forties or, at the latest, our fifties, we do begin to accept that our life is finite. We start counting off how much time, all going well, we have left. Will it be twenty years, or thirty-five or maybe more than forty? What can we accomplish in that time? Are we likely to see any great-grandchildren? How much longer can we keep playing a serve-and-volley game? Will we ever sit in the shade of the tree we just planted in the courtyard?

Heart disease and age

AGE	MALE
25–29	x 2.1
30–34	x 2.9
35–39	x 2.8
40–44	x 2.2
45–49	x 2.1
50–54	x 2.0
55–59	x 1.9
60–64	x 1.8
65–69	x 1.7

This table shows the dramatic increase in coronary heart disease with age. The death rate in each age group is presented as a ratio of the death rate in the next younger group. From the twenties to the fifties the rate doubles or, as in the thirties age group, almost triples every five years. (Source: Heart Foundation)

The statistics are against us, of course. Death rates soar in middle age. Average life expectancy may be rising, but this is more because fewer people are dying below the age of forty than because older people are living longer. A Heart Foundation survey in 1994 showed that a man's chances of dying from heart disease roughly double every five years. For instance, men in the forty to forty-four age bracket are 2.2 times more likely to die of heart disease than men in the thirty to thirty-nine bracket (see the table on page 25).

Different men react differently when confronted with these ideas of mortality. Many quickly put them at the back of their minds and carry on as before. Others undergo a change. They look back and decide to retrieve their lost youth by slimming down and becoming super fit. (This never succeeds, incidentally, so you would be wasting your time to try.) Or they look ahead and wonder how they can, one, delay death and, two, make the most of the years they're alive.

'MIDDLE AGE': A DEFINITION

Let us pause for a moment to examine this term 'middle age'. In practice, it has usually been applied to people between the ages of forty and about sixty-five, and for convenience I will generally be referring to men in this age bracket when I speak of middle age in this book. The truth is, though, that it is impossible to be too precise about the matter. By definition, the term 'middle age' is the period of life between youth and old age, so its age range must vary with the individual. It all depends on when you cease to be young (which can certainly be before forty) and when you become old. If you are resigned to being old at sixty-five, then you are certainly short-changing yourself. Science tells us that human cells are capable of living between 120 and 140 years, so there is no excuse for being old at sixty or sixty-five. Your aim must be to be middle-aged at seventy-five or eighty.

If you examine the physical decline of middle age you find that most of it has to do with movement. True, the decline shows up in all kinds of ways. As Bill Cosby said in *Time Flies*, a book he wrote about turning fifty: 'All the assorted parts of me used to be flat and hard, but in these twenty years of going downhill I have seen the growth of a gut, the thickening of thighs, the emergence of flab, the receding of a hairline and the coming forth of gas.' To this he could have added the formation of jowls, the greying of hair and the weakening of the bladder.

Because we choose to move less, the body adjusts itself to be less mobile. It starts to seize up because it is not being used often enough.

Yet the main decline, the one that really affects our daily lives, is a loss of mobility. This is partly inevitable, a consequence of aging, and partly self-induced. Because we choose to move less, the body adjusts itself to be less mobile. It starts to seize up because it is not being used often enough. The seizing up is usually worst around the middle of the body, including the lower back, which happens to be the area where middle-aged men tend to put on most of their extra weight. It also happens to be the area where most of the major organs are located, so it is definitely an area that deserves close attention.

As we all know, lower back pain is one of the great health problems afflicting our society. There was an interesting paper on the subject delivered at a National Health and Medical Research Council forum in 1998. It argued that standard methods of treatment—physiotherapy, surgery, chiropractic programs—were not working. Instead, it recommended that patients with lower back pain should be encouraged to stay as active as possible and should be reassured that in time they are likely get over the back problem naturally.

'Stay as active as possible'—this struck a chord. In fact, keeping active is the second key to healthy middle age, the first key being eating nutritious food.

THE NEED TO STAY ACTIVE

I am now extremely conscientious in doing my daily exercises, no matter what part of the world I happen to be in. Until a few years ago, I usually stopped doing them while I was away from home. Then, even if I was away for only a couple of weeks and not exercising, I would notice the difference. I felt heavier around the middle and less flexible in the lower back. My hips would start to seize up a little and my hamstrings would tighten just enough to make me feel wary about stretching out. Of course, it could be said all this was in the mind, that because I wasn't exercising I subconsciously looked for signs of impaired mobility. Whatever the truth of that, I do my exercises every day now without fail.

Shrinkage—that is, loss of height—is another sign of middle-age degeneration. It used to be thought of as an affliction of old age, but lately I have noticed men not much older than myself, men I have known for a long time, who are clearly shorter than they used to be. Some are former cricketers. I remember one old Test player who shrank before our eyes, literally. He was the great spin bowler Clarrie Grimmett, then, admittedly, in his late seventies. At Adelaide Oval there is a walkway running past the front windows of the dressing-rooms, and sitting in there we used to see Clarrie occasionally walking back and forth. Clarrie was a short man, and when he walked past you could see only the top of his head—or rather, the back of his head, because, being stooped, he had his head bent down.

Each year we would see less and less of Clarrie's head as it went past because he was getting shorter and shorter. Early one season this gave a team-mate, Ashley Mallet, an idea for a practical joke. While we were sitting in the dressing-room watching the cricket we saw a sign consisting of a piece of paper stuck to the end of a foot-long ruler go past along the bottom of the window. It read: 'Good morning fellas. I'm Clarrie Grimmett.' Ashley was crawling along the walkway with the sign held above his head.

CHAPTER FIVE
A STEP OUTSIDE THE COMFORT ZONE

Maybe you are pinning your hopes on a synthetic wonder drug without side effects fixing the problem. Forget it.

LET US ASSUME you have the desire to improve your health by changing your lifestyle. (You would hardly be reading this book otherwise.) What you must also have is the will to do it. You have to make a mental commitment to the idea of changing your lifestyle, because without that commitment you simply won't be able to do it. It will not happen of its own accord. If you are a middle-aged man who is steadily slipping into a state of inactivity and worsening health, you can be certain of one thing: nothing is going to change unless you do something about it. Maybe you are pinning your hopes on a synthetic wonder drug without side effects fixing the problem. Forget it. There isn't, nor will there ever be, such a drug.

To make this mental commitment, many men will need to be motivated in some way. They will have to be revved up psychologically before they can make a start on adopting new eating habits and getting fit. Perhaps they will need an initial emotional shove-off to get them under way. They will also need to define clearly in their own minds why they intend changing their lifestyle. It is all very well to get motivated by some fitness program you see on television and to rush out and buy a tracksuit and new walking shoes and take out a gym membership. But without a very clear idea of why you are doing it, you will not persist. You will go to the gym twice, feel stiff and sore afterwards, wonder why on earth you are punishing yourself like this, throw the new walking shoes in the cupboard, put your gym membership card in the bottom drawer and forget all about it.

So have a definite goal in mind. Have it fixed in your head that you are changing your lifestyle to ensure you are healthy, fit and supple enough to work on the hobby farm you intend retiring to after you turn sixty—or whatever your motivation happens to be. The goal may be short-term. You may simply wish to avoid the embarrassment of being asked to join a game of volleyball at a barbeque, knowing that in your present state you will look ridiculous if you try to dash about, huffing and puffing, with a big belly bulging over your shorts. If you fear this—if you think you are likely to miss the first ball that comes your way and fall flat on your face—the chances are you will refuse to join the game. In other words, your options in life are reduced.

It is another thing entirely to motivate someone to embark on a change of lifestyle that is meant to last a lifetime.

Motivation can provide the shove-off, but I am afraid it cannot provide more than that. Over the years I have listened to some of the best motivational speakers in Australia, men of the calibre of Ron Barassi, Laurie Lawrence and Alan Jones. I learned a great deal from each of them, but I cannot say any of them really motivated me. Rather, they gave me the information I needed to motivate myself. It is one thing for a football coach to fire up his players and make them believe they can run through brick walls for the hour or two they are on the field. It is another thing entirely to motivate someone to embark on a change of lifestyle that is meant to last a lifetime.

My hope is that this book will provide readers with the motivation for getting started, and then the information they need to keep going. To keep going, though, they must have made the solid mental commitment to the change that I spoke about earlier. So although this book may inspire someone to start eating more vegetables and less meat tomorrow, unless he understands why he is doing it and, therefore, really wants to do it he is unlikely to persevere with his new eating habits for more than a week or two.

Motivation to get started

The impetus to do something about your health can come from various sources. Recently, the distinguished Adelaide-based author and cosmologist Paul Davies was asked what inspired him to actively protect his health. He replied, 'My motivation? I have seen many colleagues, the same age or even younger, simply drop dead from a heart attack.' In other words, his motivation was the fear of dying in middle age (Davies is now in his early fifties). He changed his eating habits and began exercising daily. Now, he works out for about forty-five minutes every weekday morning. 'I find I function better from keeping reasonably fit,' Davies said. 'I think more clearly, I achieve more and I am a happier person.'

My main motivation as a cricketer was the knowledge that the pain of failure lasts a lot longer than the pain of success.

Sometimes the motivation can be more subtle. I once heard of a boy at my son's school who had been chubby for years yet continued to ignore the advice his parents gave him about losing weight. Then, one day, while he was in his early teens he suddenly changed his lifestyle. He stopped eating junk food and drinking milkshakes, and he started doing laps of the local oval. His surprised parents wondered why. It later emerged that a girl he had a liking for had called him 'fatty'. He obviously knew he was overweight, but hearing the word 'fatty' immediately changed his perception of himself. He was wounded badly enough by it to want to take some action.

Maybe the initiative has been taken by your wife. She is changing her lifestyle and you have decided to join her. Or maybe you have had a heart attack or been diagnosed with diabetes and your doctor has warned you that unless you take radical steps to improve your health you have a very bleak future. It is a pity more doctors are not as blunt as this with their patients when they need to be. A genuine health scare can jolt just about anyone into action.

We can probably all think of a middle-aged man we know who is prudent in other ways yet for some reason resists the idea of trying to improve his health. Such an attitude seems to defy explanation. If you are in your twenties you may be excused for thinking that you will enjoy good health forever. When you are middle-aged, though, you feel mortality closing in. You cannot ignore the symptoms of aging. Yet many men do seem to ignore them. Why?

I suspect these men already see themselves as being past it. In their minds they have resigned themselves to the physical decline they associate with middle age. They think to themselves: 'Well, I'm getting on, and I'm going to have aches and ailments, and I'm going to be less mobile than I was. There's nothing much I can do about it, so I might as well cop it.' In short, they give in.

My own experience leads me to believe that such men have a poor self-image. It is because they have a negative view of themselves that they are willing to accept increasing ill health and loss of mobility as their lot in life. Conversely, I have also found that men who do make an effort to improve their health and fitness also develop a more positive self-image.

THE FEAR FACTOR

Fear is a common denominator in all this. From childhood onwards, fear prevents people doing a lot of things they would like to do or feel they should do. It may be fear of rejection, or fear of looking stupid in front of friends, or fear of failure. Some of the fear may be inculcated. We use fear as a deterrent to our children: 'Don't do that—you might get hurt.'

Parents around the world say this to their children every day. All of us have had certain fears buried in our subconscious since we were children. Most of us will never get rid of them, of course—which is a great pity, for they certainly prevent us realising our full potential.

From childhood onwards, fear prevents people doing a lot of things they would like to do or feel they should do.

The fear factor can be present in everything we do, but it is especially evident on the sporting field. Sometimes it is fear of success. I am sure there are a number of world-ranked golfers who are delighted to be in the top twenty in the world but who have no desire to be in the top three. One of them told me so a few years ago. He was content to be up near the top, enjoying all the benefits, financial and otherwise, of being a top player, while being spared all the pressures of being at the top. The fear of those pressures deterred him from striving to be the best, and, considering how severe those pressures can be, you could not blame him for that.

In cricket, fear is an enormous influence on how players perform. Even those of us who made it to the top were constantly beset by fears. Don Bradman would have been beset by them, too, but he apparently handled them better than the rest of us. Every time you go in to bat you run a high risk of failure—you risk looking an idiot. In fact, the chance of failure in cricket is statistically much greater than the chance of success. This is not easy to live with, especially since a batsman's failure is such a public event. It is not a pleasant experience to be out for a duck and have to make the long walk back, knowing that the mob are chuckling to themselves over your misfortune.

I could not count the number of cricketers I saw who were ideally equipped, physically, to become outstanding international cricketers but who never made the grade, the main reason being, in my view, a fear of some kind. Fear of failure, fear of injury, fear of success, fear of having to leave the comfort zone—that is, of being torn away from their support system. They might have been great players on their home ground, but take them to another city or, more particularly, take them overseas and they would prove unequal to the task.

> If I have learned anything about life it is this: to achieve anything you must be prepared to move out of the comfort zone. You must be prepared to be different, to have a go. A lot of people, I am sure, are afraid of the consequences of making a change to their lives. They fear that their workmates, or friends, or even their children will think they have gone loopy.

It is fear that stops people moving out of the comfort zone. Of course, being in the comfort zone is very pleasant. It is easy to come home, have dinner and sit in front of the television until you go to bed. There is a particular show on Monday night that you have to watch, then another on Tuesday, and so on. If you want to get out of that routine, perhaps it is fear of some consequence or other that holds you back. If you wish to change your life, though, you must move out of the comfort zone, and to do this you are going to have to make changes to your routine which, initially at least, may not be comfortable.

This is why it is vitally important for you to have a strong motivation to do what you set out to do (in this case, to change your style of eating and change your daily routine to include some kind of exercise), because you will need that motivation to carry you on past the barriers you will surely find in your way. Your wife may not want to change the cooking habits of a lifetime; your children will probably not want to eat the same food as you; your friends will think you've gone mad because you aren't eating the same food that you've eaten before. They will all want to be dragging you back into your comfort zone, not only for your sake but for their own. The mere fact *you* have stepped outside the zone is threatening *their* place in the zone, too.

...the first burst of criticism you receive will set you back and make you start thinking whether it is all worthwhile.

PSYCHOLOGICAL BARRIERS

If you do not have a strong motivation, it is likely that the first burst of criticism you receive will set you back and make you start thinking whether it is all worthwhile. You may not give up then, but you are sure to give up sooner or later in the face of criticism because it will all seem too painful, too uncomfortable. There are psychological barriers around all of us which we never wish to push against, because by doing so we stand out from the crowd and that feels uncomfortable. We do not want to be seen to be different. We do not want to be criticised. We certainly do not want to be ridiculed. The easiest thing is to stop pushing and sink back into the comfort zone.

I remember a few occasions early in my cricket career when the stress of competition got to me. I would be out there batting under pressure in difficult conditions and I would think to myself: this is just too hard; things would be a lot easier back in the dressing-room. More than once, this kind of thinking caused a lapse of concentration and I was dismissed soon afterwards. Back in the dressing-room, my attitude changed at once. I longed to be out there again, soaking up the stress and strain, and ending the day with some runs on the board. As it was, I no longer had any pressure on me, but I did not have the runs on the board, either.

> If you set out to change your lifestyle for the betterment of your health, you are sure, sooner or later, to come to a barrier you will need to break through. Only after breaking through it will you be able to put in the hard work that produces the benefits for your health and wellbeing.

My main motivation as a cricketer was the knowledge that the pain of failure lasts a lot longer than the pain of success. Even in such a protracted game as cricket, a batsman who makes a century rarely has to endure hardship for more than three or fours hours. If he is out for a duck, though, he can brood about the failure for weeks. After scoring a century in a Test match people would say to me what a thrill this must have been for me. In fact, my chief emotional reaction on reaching a hundred was always one of relief—relief at not having failed.

So the fear of failure can be used as a positive motivation. By all means, use it to push on with the health program you have mapped out for yourself. If your resolve weakens, think hard about how badly you will feel about it later if you give up now—and of the great opportunity for revitalising your life which will have gone begging.

CHAPTER SIX
MELLOWING OR MENOPAUSE?

By knowing how far you've already gone downhill physically, you ought to be more determined to make sure the slide does not continue.

MUCH HAS BEEN written lately about so-called male menopause. It is suggested that in middle age men experience hormonal changes, not unlike those that cause menopause in women, which can affect them both physically and psychologically. A lot more research needs to be done before we really understand the process, but there is no doubt that a sizeable proportion of middle-aged men undergo a change in personality. It seems to happen most often in the fifties, although the process can begin as early as twenty-five. Typically, these men cease to be as vital as they were before. They are vaguer, less interested in the conversation going on around them, less prepared to argue for a point of view, more willing to accommodate others' wishes and demands (not necessarily a bad thing), less likely to do anything the slightest bit out of the ordinary. In short, much of the fight has gone out of them.

...what is the point of living longer if you are not extending the period of life in which you are active?

At its best, this can be viewed simply as mellowing with age. At its worst, it can be considered a degenerative process in which a man's vital personality slowly drains away. In my view it ought to be consciously resisted, and there is a good reason for that. The big danger in becoming more passive and less decisive in personality is that it can trigger off a general decline, physically and mentally, in middle age. When a man's personality softens, everything else is liable to soften too, and he will be more likely to surrender to age in all kinds of ways. The ravages of middle age will soon overtake him.

If this softening of personality is a purely natural process, as the evidence suggests, it cannot be prevented. I am sure, though, that it can be delayed. If you can keep yourself in good physical health and fitness and maintain a good, positive frame of mind, there is no reason why, with a bit of conscious effort, you should not retain the personality you developed as a young man (or the better elements of it, anyway) into old age. After all, this same combination of good health, good fitness and positive outlook is certainly successful in resisting the onset of other symptoms of aging that are traditionally associated with middle age.

The American golfer Jack Nicklaus is a shining example of a person who has preserved his mental vigour. He deserved to be cheered by middle-aged men everywhere when he finished fifth in the 1998 US Masters at the age of fifty-eight. To have had enough golfing skill at fifty-eight to finish so close to the top in one of the world's premier tournaments was truly remarkable. But it was even more remarkable, in my opinion, to be still strong enough mentally to do it.

MIDLIFE CHANGES

Not long ago a survey by the Australian Bureau of Statistics reported a sharp rise in the number of middle-aged men who were intending to give up work earlier than they needed to for the specific purpose of having more time to indulge in leisure activities. The survey focused on men over the age of forty-five who were intending to retire early, and as many as 57 per cent of them said that a desire for more leisure time was their chief motivation. This is consistent with a recent trend for middle-aged men in Australia (and probably in most Western countries) to make decisions affecting their lives that are based on 'lifestyle choices' rather than 'career choices'. In other words, they are shaping their lives to suit their personal inclinations. We have all heard of instances of this: the doctor who gives up his practice and becomes a winegrower, the press photographer who takes over a city pub, the chartered accountant who leaves the city to run a Blue Mountains guesthouse.

In my experience, these midlife changes can sometimes be unsuccessful and the men who make them end up returning to their former professions. This is not to say that changes of life are necessarily a mistake. On the contrary, they show that the man concerned has not allowed himself to stagnate. Yet I suspect that in a lot of cases the midlife changes are caused by a variation of male menopause. The men concerned sense that the years are racing by and that they are running out of time. Furthermore, they reason that if they are ever going to make the break and head in a new direction they must do it now. If they wait until the retirement age, sixty-five, they will be too old.

Although this may well be true, the observation needs to be made that by taking control of our health now we should all be able to extend our vigorous middle age long beyond sixty-five. After all, what is the point of living longer if you are not extending the period of life in which you are active? All you end up doing is spending more years in a state of aged infirmity. I made the point earlier that keeping the twin evils of cancer and heart disease at bay was not my main concern when I decided to do something about improving my health. I was more interested in delaying the general physical deterioration associated with middle age, which, as we all know, can make men of fifty or sixty look and behave like old men.

Already an Old Man

Everyone reading this will know someone of this kind. He is, let's say, fifty-five years old. He has a pot belly of long standing and has begun to form jowls around his neck. His shoulders look withered under his shirt and his arms and legs have begun to waste away through lack of exercise. He has trouble bending down over his belly to tie his shoelaces. He even has trouble twisting his neck to look backwards while reversing his car. All his movements are heavy and laboured. You can hardly blame him for this, though, for most of his joints are stiff or sore or both. In short, he has ceased to be a vibrant, vigorous male. Subconsciously, he has given in to the aging process. He has succumbed to male menopause.

Consciously, though, he may still think of himself as virile and attractive. The 55-year-old man I have just described may still turn out in smart gear. His hair may be well groomed and he may even wear a gold chain around his neck. In my experience, this is a common paradox of aging. Long after men allow themselves to sink into a state of decrepitude, they still think of themselves as young and virile. The mental image they have of themselves is altogether different from the real thing.

An acquaintance a few years older than myself told me recently how shocked he had been a few days earlier to see himself on a security monitor in a liquor shop. Without warning, he was confronted with a side-on view of a sagging, pear-shaped person. He'd had no idea he looked like that. He scarcely recognised himself. In his mind, he still looked more or less like the man he had been fifteen years or more earlier.

So a clear and accurate image of yourself is a useful asset if you are thinking of trying to get fit and healthy. By knowing how far you've already gone downhill physically, you ought to be more determined to make sure the slide does not continue.

CHAPTER SEVEN
THE STEP-BY-STEP APPROACH

It is safer to change your lifestyle in stages. Set yourself modest goals to start with.

BY SOME MEANS, THEN, you have made the mental commitment to transform your lifestyle. If you possess an iron will, you may be able to make all the necessary changes at once. In my experience, going cold turkey like this is difficult. The danger is you will not be able to stick to the new regime you set yourself and then give up on it completely. If that happens, you are worse off than when you started, because you will find it hard to work up the enthusiasm to try again.

It is safer to change your lifestyle in stages. Set yourself modest goals to start with. The goals shouldn't be too small, because you won't feel you are getting anywhere. But they must not be so big that you cannot feel absolutely confident of attaining them.

The advantage of this step-by-step approach is that you can monitor your progress. Once you have reached one target, you can set off confidently for the next. I used to do this when I was batting. Making a century is every batsman's objective, but at the start of an innings I found a hundred runs much too distant a goal to aim for. Instead, I used to set myself targets of ten runs at a time, because I always felt I was capable of making ten. So on arriving at the crease my first aim was to make ten. Then I aimed for twenty. Then thirty, and so on. The beauty of this was that each time I completed another ten runs I had a reason to give myself a mental pat on the back and I also had a starting point from which to aim for the next goal.

As a first step you could decide to take action on three fronts.

One:

Cut a limited number of fatty foods—say, cheese, fried chips and ice-cream—from your normal diet.

Two:

If you are in the habit of drinking every day, make one day a week an alcohol-free day.

Three:

If you have been doing little or no exercise, set yourself a modest fitness program you can stick to. Make it a rule for yourself that you walk for twenty minutes twice a week. Or rejoin the tennis group and play one day a week.

Reaching your first target will certainly give you a psychological boost. There is nothing more uplifting than success. By then you ought to be feeling fitter and more energetic and be starting to lose a little weight. You should be fired up with determination to take the next step. What should this second step be? Again, it is for you to decide. Maybe start eliminating one or two red meat meals entirely. Another idea is to replace all fried vegetables with steamed or boiled vegetables. Start walking three times a week instead of two.

The less you try to change your eating habits at any one time, the better your chances of changing them. Your general aim should be to reduce your intake of protein, especially animal protein, and reduce your intake of fat. So basically you ought to be looking to cut back on meat, cheese and all other dairy foods. Simultaneously, you need to increase the quantity of vegetables and fresh fruit (not out of a can) that you eat.

Once again, precisely how you accomplish this is up to you. You probably have a wife and children who will be eating at the same table at the same time, and obviously you will need to fit in with them. I know from experience the problems that can arise when different members of the family disagree on the choice of food. While it is pointless to suggest detailed menus here (experience suggests that nobody follows detailed menus, anyway), the following lists may be useful as a guide:

- ***You need to eat more steamed or boiled vegetables, fresh fruit and grain foods such as bread.***
- ***You need to eat less meat (including sausages), cheese, milk, fried vegetables, eggs, ice-cream, cream biscuits, fast food of all kinds.***
- ***If your evening meal normally consists of meat and vegetables, have less meat and more vegetables.***

You will be eating a modified meal rather than a radically different one, so there will be less stress on you. There will also be less stress on the rest of your family, who may well resent having a revolutionary diet imposed on them.

So begin your campaign for better health not by launching an all-out assault on your eating habits but by picking off smaller targets one by one.

- ***Cut out margarine on everything but toast—have jam or honey on your bread and cottage cheese on your sandwiches.***
- ***Cook with skim yoghurt instead of cream.***
- ***Have one scoop of ice-cream on your dessert, not two.***
- ***Avoid cheese whenever possible.***
- ***Avoid bacon whenever possible.***

If you are hungry between meals, eat a piece of fruit instead of the usual snack. Indeed, you might make this the very starting point of your change in eating habits—that is, eliminate the poor food you eat between meals (biscuits, bars of chocolate and the like) and replace it with good food, especially fruit. When playing golf I am constantly surprised at how many men will stop halfway to buy a chocolate bar, supposedly because the chocolate gives them energy. If they do need energy, chocolate is about the last thing they ought to be eating. Or they stop and down a soft drink. This is another food item you could begin by eliminating. Have a glass of water or juice (sugar-free brands only) instead.

None of us drink enough water. We ought to be drinking a couple of litres a day. If you start to feel thirsty, you are already dehydrated, and dehydration can be harmful. Much better to drink small quantities of water throughout the day.

Naturally it is a lot easier to control what you eat in your own kitchen. Make all the changes there and for the time being don't worry too much about what you eat when you go out. Sure, if you do have the tenacity to stick to your new eating habits when you go out that's fine, but don't try sticking to them at your next business lunch or the next dinner party you are invited to if this is going to stress you out. Do your best, though, to avoid fatty food and watch the volume. Remember, less is better.

New habits

What we are really talking about when we talk of changing our lifestyle is replacing old habits with new habits. The experts say it takes twenty-one days to change a habit, so some patience and perseverance are needed. The trick is making sure you don't get fed up with your new eating habits before they become ingrained, which is why I warn against being too tough on yourself to begin with.

As soon as one set of new eating habits have been formed, though, you can move on and set yourself new goals. Perhaps you are ready now to cut out some red meat dishes entirely. Or to cut out ice-cream entirely.

The experts say it takes twenty-one days to change a habit, so some patience and perseverance are needed.

Or to start experimenting with vegetable curries. Or to swear off junk food completely. Whatever goals you choose, make sure they are achievable. Then, when these goals are attained, set yourself some more. In this way, you can improve your eating habits stage by stage, as if by a kind of ratchet effect.

The lifestyle changes you need to make are going to take time. It has taken you forty, fifty or more years to reach the state of health—or ill health—that you are in today. All this cannot be undone overnight.

There is no quick fix, but there is certainly a fix. The recuperative powers of the body are one of the wonders of nature. Unlike the clapped-out car that has been left to rust, your clapped-out body need not be a wreck bound for the scrapyard. It can regenerate—provided you provide it with the right fuel. It can regain health, shape and vigour. It is entirely up to you.

The way ahead may not be short (allow yourself two years to reach optimum health and fitness) and at times it will require from you considerable perseverance. What I can promise—and I invite the most cynical readers of this book to accept this as fact—is that the difference in how you feel at the end of it all will make any difficulties you encounter along the way seem unimportant.

CHAPTER EIGHT
LIKE FATHER, LIKE SON

You can look at your father today and be pretty sure you are seeing the kind of man you are destined to be in twenty-five years' time if you continue to live the way he lived.

I ONCE HEARD A JOKE about an old (or perhaps middle-aged) farmer who lived in a remote corner of Ireland where even the simplest modern conveniences were unknown. One day he made a rare visit to the nearest village and passed a market stall where someone was selling hand mirrors. The farmer had never seen or heard of a mirror before, so he stopped, picked one up and looked at his reflection. 'Heavens!' he said. 'It's a picture of my father!' I cannot remember how the joke ended, but I do remember this part of it because it rang true with me. Typically, as a man gets on in years, he finds himself becoming more and more like his father as he remembers him from boyhood days. When we are young, we find it impossible to imagine we could ever end up looking and behaving like our middle-aged fathers, yet most of us do.

So in a sense our fathers live again in us. This is true in more ways than one. The way our own fathers lived their lives—what they ate, how

Most people acquire their eating habits from their parents and keep them for as long as they live.

much they drank, how carefully they looked after their health—certainly influences us one way or another. Unless we make a conscious decision to do otherwise, most of us do what our fathers did.

It is sometimes said that whether or not you enjoy good health is determined not by any choices you make yourself but by a choice that was made for you by fate—namely, which father and mother you were born to. In other words, the theory that health is largely a matter of genetics.

It is true that parents have a huge bearing on their children's health in later years, although not only for reasons of genetics. Imitation plays a big part, too. Children copy many of the things their parents do, and there isn't one thing they copy more closely than their parents' style of eating. Most people acquire their eating habits from their parents and keep them for as long as they live. They eat the style of food in later life that they ate as children at home. This is why nutrition in the family home is so important: not only your own health but the health of your children for years to come depends on it.

For Judy and me, the fact that we had three children was an extra incentive to adopt a new style of eating. We wanted to do the best by them healthwise, so we became very conscious not only of what we were putting into our mouths but of what we were putting into their mouths, too.

My own father, Martin, never changed his eating habits, and in middle age became increasingly less healthy. I played golf with him when he visited us in Brisbane in 1983, and all around the course I had to wait for him to catch up with me. He was breathing heavily, which I regarded as a worrying sign. He blamed it on a recent bout of flu, but I pleaded with him to see a doctor when he returned to Adelaide. He promised me he would, and he did—although I suspect he told the doctor he had just been suffering from flu and the doctor accepted it. This was not the first time I had urged Dad to do something about his health. Over the previous three or four years I had talked to him about the need to do some exercise and to modify his eating habits. He listened politely, but I'm sure he did nothing.

He died of heart disease only a few months later, aged sixty-four. It was a tragically shortened life. My father may have had some small warnings along the way, angina pains and the like, but if so he never told anyone about them. The first big warning he received proved to be his last.

I was with him that day. I happened to be visiting Adelaide for a friend's fortieth birthday, and Dad and I went out early in the morning to play golf. On arriving at the course we found there was a ladies event about to start, but we were allowed to hit off ahead of them. Two other men had turned up to play, so we were grouped together as a four. Playing as a four slowed us down, and we were under pressure from the women following fast behind us in pairs. Dad was struggling to keep up and after four or five holes he pulled out and returned to sit in the car. I had played a few more holes when a club official rode over on a motorbike to say my father was ill. I ran back and found Dad in a bad way. He was leaning against the

> ***What happened to my father made me realise that it is better to take action to improve our health while we are still healthy than to wait until we are given an ultimatum.***

car, obviously in a lot of pain.

I drove him, via a doctor's surgery, to hospital, where he was admitted and diagnosed as having had a heart attack. I visited him in the cardiac ward that evening, just as the meal trolleys were being wheeled about, and found him sitting up in bed. I could not believe the dinner being served. Everything on the tray ought to have been on the banned list for heart patients. There was a mushy meat dish with mashed potatoes and bedraggled vegetables, plus a bowl of ice-cream and some sugary biscuits. I was staggered, but Dad didn't mind. It was the kind of food he liked. I took the tray away from him and complained to a doctor. It would not really have mattered to Dad if he had eaten that meal, of course, but it said a great deal about attitudes to health that a hospital should be serving it.

I am sure the reason my father could not bring himself to change his lifestyle in those last few years was that it simply seemed too hard. He was approaching his mid-sixties, and I suppose he reasoned that any damage his diet might do to him had already been done. I could not agree with this, for I strongly believe it is never too late to turn your health around, but I could understand it. At the same time, what happened to my father made me realise that it is better to take action to improve our health while we are still healthy than to wait until we are given an ultimatum by a doctor in years to come, by which time we probably won't have the will to do it anyway.

HEALTH LESSONS FROM OUR FATHERS

We can all learn a lot about health from our fathers. Let us assume you eat the same kind of food and follow roughly the same kind of lifestyle as your father did. Suppose you are forty-five and he is seventy. You can look at your father today and be pretty sure you are seeing the kind of man you are destined to be in twenty-five years' time if you continue to live the way he lived. If you like what you see—if you would be content at seventy to be just like your father is now— then you are very fortunate. You are also in a small minority. Most men of seventy are slower, heavier, stiffer in the joints and afflicted with more health conditions than they need to be at their age. So chances are you would like to be fitter and healthier than your father is now. You would probably want to have a better body shape and posture than his and be plagued by fewer aches and pains. You would naturally wish to be spared the indigestion (another common affliction of middle age), which you see him suffering. You would almost certainly wish to be more active and agile. You would want to stride out when you go for a walk, instead of sauntering along; to bend down easily to pick something from the floor; to play with your grandchildren instead of just watching them play.

My grandfather Vic Richardson played cricket for Australia; in fact, he captained the Australian team. So as boys we would have been thrilled if he had joined us in the backyard to bowl a few balls or have a hit. Unfortunately, Vic was never too willing, and, having played a lot of cricket myself, I can understand that the idea of playing cricket with kids in the backyard would not have had a lot of appeal. Still, I sincerely hope that if I live long enough to have grandchildren and they want me to join them in a backyard cricket match I will both have the desire to do it and be active enough to be able to do it.

How healthy do you feel?

	Age group (years)					
Self-assessed health status	*15–24*	*25–34*	*35–44*	*45–64*	*65–74*	*75 +*
Excellent	280.6	209.3	193.7	180.7	113.0	97.4
Very good	399.1	417.5	406.6	306.4	220.8	182.7
Good	237.4	277.4	285.1	309.0	321.6	283.8
Fair	75.7	82.7	90.1	150.2	231.5	283.8
Poor	7.2	13.2	24.5	53.7	113.1	152.4
TOTAL	1,000.0	1,000.0	1,000.0	1,000.0	1,000.0	1,000.0

This table was part of the National Health Survey by the Australian Bureau of Statistics, released at the end of 1996. A total of 8997 men of all ages were asked to assess the state of their own health. As the results show, men steadily feel less healthy as they grow older.

CHAPTER NINE
Vegetarian by Chance

... my personal experience may encourage you to move some of the way towards a vegetarian diet by replacing a few meat-based meals each week with vegetarian meals.

I BECAME A VEGETARIAN almost by chance. In 1993 my wife, Judy, decided to go on a forty-day cleansing diet (see page 175) and, partly to give her support, I offered to join her. The diet happened to be meat-free and dairy-free, but we did not think of it specifically as a vegetarian diet. Although both of us had given up dairy products entirely and red meat almost entirely many years earlier, we had not given any thought to the idea of becoming pure vegetarians before we tried the diet. Our intention was to do the cleansing and get what benefit we could from it, then revert to our usual eating habits and perhaps do the cleansing again in a few years' time.

At the end of the forty days Judy and I looked at each other and said, 'How good do you feel!' We both felt terrific—so terrific that we decided there and then to eat pure vegetarian food thereafter. The change that a

I enjoyed the flavours and I enjoyed the variety. Most of all I enjoyed my new feeling of wellbeing.

meatless diet produced in us was striking. Instead of feeling weighed down after a meal, I felt light. For the first time in my life I really enjoyed eating food. I enjoyed the texture of the food, I enjoyed the flavours and I enjoyed the variety. Most of all I enjoyed my new feeling of wellbeing.

It was a sensation which even now I find hard to put into words. The difference in how I felt was so profound that I could never consider reverting to a meat diet. I could never go back. It isn't that I am physically incapable now of stomaching roast lamb or a mixed grill. If someone were to put a steak in front of me tomorrow and threaten to shoot me unless I ate it, then, sure, I could do it. I did not become a pure vegetarian because of any sense of revulsion at the idea of eating a dead animal's flesh. I did it with the entirely selfish motive of wanting to be healthier.

Having said this, let me make it clear again that I expect few of the people who read this book to become fully fledged vegetarians. The vegetarian style of eating has worked so well for me, however, that I feel obliged to at least present the evidence in its favour.

> If nothing else, my personal experience may encourage you to move some of the way towards a vegetarian diet by replacing a few meat-based meals each week with vegetarian meals. The further you move in this direction, the better off you will be healthwise.

Plant foods and health

Why is plant-based food healthier? The simple answer is that virtually everything about plant food is good for you. Plant foods consist essentially of protein, carbohydrate and (except in the case of coconuts) unsaturated fat. They contain plenty of fibre, usually little or no fat, no cholesterol and an abundance of vitamins and antioxidants. By contrast, although meat and dairy foods contain things that are good for you, they also contain many things that are bad. They consist essentially of protein and saturated fat. They are hard for the body to digest, and they contain no fibre at all. Another unpleasant fact about meat is that it putrefies inside you. In fact, an animal's flesh starts to decompose as soon as the animal is killed. Moreover, meat acidifies the system, whereas plant foods in the raw state have the opposite effect.

The statistics

The statistics bear this out. They show that vegetarians are slimmer, more energetic, less prone to disease and more likely to live longer. This was highlighted when the Australian Cancer Society launched its *Lifetrack 2000* dietary guide in July 1998. One of the society's senior epidemiologists, Dr Graham Giles, pointed to the fact that one in two cancers are caused by diet. He made an interesting comparison with smoking. Although smoking is universally recognised as a terrible danger to health, the truth is it is not as dangerous to health as eating badly.

Whereas smoking was the cause of 30 per cent of cancers, Dr Giles said, inferior diets were the cause of between 40 and 60 per cent. Dr Giles then cited a telling fact. He said that vegetarians were about 35 per cent less likely to develop cancer than meat-eaters. I thought this was a pretty impressive statistic. It seemed to me that if someone could come up with a pill that reduced the risk of cancer to this extent, everyone would be taking it.

Not long ago Roger French, the natural health editor of the excellent Australian magazine *New Vegetarian and Natural Health*, published two interesting tables, one comparing plant foods with animal products, and the other, plant-eating animals with carnivores. Both tables got their message across so succinctly that I have reproduced them in this book on pages 64 and 65. The comparison between carnivores and plant-eaters is intriguing. Roger French wrote: 'Human anatomy is distinctly different from that of the carnivore animals. It is very close to that of our cousins, the mainly vegetarian apes, including gorillas. There is no doubt that our bodies are designed to handle diets that are basically vegetarian.' French added: 'Meat is little more than second-hand grass. We need our nutrients first-hand.'

Right up to the time Judy and I went on the forty-day diet I still felt the same resistance to pure vegetarianism I had always felt. I had heard all the stories about the inadequacies of vegetarian food, and I suppose I wanted to believe most of them. I certainly believed that it was not a balanced diet, that if we did not eat some meat we would be undernourished and would risk becoming anaemic. I found it hard to imagine how I could ever enjoy food again if meat was entirely eliminated from the menu. It seemed to me that becoming a pure vegetarian meant depriving myself permanently of one of life's great pleasures. It also seemed somehow un-Australian.

ANTI-VEGETARIAN PREJUDICE

I shared the popular prejudice against vegetarians themselves. I thought of them as a fringe minority. They were people who subscribed to strange beliefs, like members of a cult. In Eastern cultures, the vegetarian movement happens to be closely allied with spiritual beliefs. Unfortunately, this idea has spilled over into Western culture and distorted the image the public has of vegetarians. As a result, in the eyes of many Australians, becoming a vegetarian does not just mean adopting a new style of eating; rather, it means adopting a whole new, rather weird style of living.

This was certainly how I thought of vegetarians. They were alternative-lifestyle people. They wore sandals, beards and ponytails and burned incense in their homes. Or, otherwise, they were self-righteous types who seemed to think they were somehow superior to us ordinary meat-eaters and who caused inconvenience for everyone at lunches and dinner parties.

The truth, I now realise, is that I had never known any vegetarians personally. To the best of my knowledge, none of the people I mixed with up to that time was a vegetarian, and I feel safe in saying that not one of the men I played with in almost eighteen years of top-level cricket was a vegetarian. If any of them were, they certainly did not ask for special food at the lunch break. Some of the Indian cricketers we played against must have been vegetarians, although they never made the fact known to any of us. In fact, the man who planned the forty-day diet for us, Joseph Oros, was the first person I came into close contact with whom I knew to be a vegetarian, and I did not meet him until I was nearly forty-five years old.

As I write this, it has been five years since I became a vegetarian. What difference has it made to me? One difference is that I eat a much smaller quantity of food. In fact, I estimate I now eat about one third of the volume of food I ate before. The other obvious difference is that I feel better. I know my health is better. This has shown up in surprising ways. The eighteen years I spent in the sun playing first-class cricket took a terrible toll of my skin and left me with an apparently incurable skin infection. The vegetarian diet fixed it. Not only has my skin condition disappeared but many of the lesions and scar tissue that were already there have gone, too. Moreover, whereas I was having ten to fifteen sun spots burned off my face and body every year, since becoming a vegetarian I have had only one burned off.

Although I use the term 'vegetarian diet', it is not one I am completely comfortable with. To me, a 'diet' is an eating regime that lasts a short time only. The term 'diet' also has a bit of a stigma attached to it, because over the years many so-called diets have been discredited. It is better to say, simply, that I have changed my style of eating: I have changed my eating habits.

Sometimes when people speak to me about my preference for vegetarian food I sense that they regard me as a masochist. They know I have given up many of the foods that they enjoy most, so they assume I am living a life of mortification and self-denial. This amuses me. I have never in my life enjoyed food so much as I have since becoming a vegetarian. Nor have I ever looked forward so much to meals as I do now.

Why? Well, in the first place, I enjoy the taste of food more than I ever did, and this is because the taste of the vegetables, fruits or whatever else is on the plate is the natural taste. Over the years I have eaten in many of the big-name restaurants around the world, and the fact is that even at these places you rarely taste the food itself. What you taste are the sauces they put with it.

MEAT: REMEMBERED BUT NOT MISSED

I have not missed the taste of a single meat dish. I don't miss the flavours of any of the foods, including cheeses, I have since given up. Possibly this is because I did not relish the taste of meat quite as much as some people apparently do. What can be said with certainty is that not once in all the time I have been a vegetarian have I had any desire to eat the meat dishes I used to eat.

One of the main reasons meat-eaters are reluctant to try vegetarian food is that they have it fixed in their heads eating vegetarian is something you do for health not for pleasure. This is nonsense. I can honestly say that if vegetarian food had no health benefits at all I would still eat vegetarian by choice. It is hard to believe that anyone who enjoys good food would not enjoy the flavours, the aromas, the mixtures, the variety, the novelty of vegetarian food. We have all heard people say their mouths watered at the prospect of eating a certain meal. When I was eating meat I never had that sensation. Since becoming a vegetarian I have had it regularly.

Differences between flesh and plant foods

Flesh Foods

- *Essentially protein and saturated fat*
- *Highly acid-forming in the body*
- *Contain no fibre, hence long transit time in bowel and putrefaction*
- *Contain cholesterol and cause it to be made in the body*
- *Form excessive uric acid (causing gout)*
- *High in food chain, so high in pollutants (eg. mercury in tuna)*
- *May be contaminated with hormones, antibiotics and vaccines*
- *Contain fear toxins produced at slaughter*
- *Contain the toxic wastes normally present in animal tissues*
- *Begin to decompose at animal's death*
- *Encourage unhealthy putrefactive bacteria in our intestines*

Plant Foods

- *Essentially protein, carbohydrate and unsaturated fat*
- *Fruit and vegetables are alkali-forming in the body*
- *Contain abundant fibre, so short transit time and good regularity*
- *Contain no cholesterol*
- *Cause much less uric acid to form*
- *All at bottom of food chain, so lower pesticide residues*
- *Free of antibiotics and vaccines*
- *Don't putrefy*
- *Encourage the vital 'friendly' gut bacteria (which digest fibre, manufacture vitamin B12 and so on)*

Differences in anatomy between carnivores and vegetarians

Carnivores

- *Most have retractable claws and long teeth for holding and killing prey*
- *Have very short bowels for rapid expulsion of putrefactive bacteria associated with decomposing flesh*
- *Have jaws which open only in an up and down motion*
- *Do not sweat through the skin but control body heat by extruding the tongue and rapid breathing*
- *Their saliva lacks ptyalin and cannot pre-digest starches*
- *Secrete up to 10 times stronger hydrochloric acid than vegetarians, sufficient to dissolve bones*
- *Lap water like a cat*

Vegetarians

- *Don't have claws; have grinding teeth for crushing plant foods*
- *Have very long bowels for supporting the fermentative bacteria involved in the digestion of plant foods*
- *Have jaws which can move sideways for chewing*
- *Have sweat pores for heat control and the elimination of impurities*
- *Have the enzyme, ptyalin, in the saliva for the pre-digestion of starches*
- *Have less acid and cannot consume bones*
- *Drink by suction*

(Source: *New Vegetarian and Natural Health*)

The point was made before that I did not become a vegetarian, as some others do, because of any feeling of revulsion at the thought of eating dead flesh. Several years on, however, I have begun to develop a philosophical aversion to eating meat. I do not feel passionately enough about it to become an activist, so you will never see me protesting outside an abattoir somewhere, but I do have an ethical objection to killing and eating animals when it is obvious that we are much better off going to the food source ourselves. The animals in this context are an unnecessary 'middle man' between humans and plant life.

My views on the matter are also coloured by the knowledge that the animals we raise for the table are treated very badly through intensive farming methods. Nowadays, when I drive past a chicken factory, piggery, or even past a cattle property, I sense an emotional response within myself which was not there before.

There are other factors to consider when deciding to give up meat which need not be delved into here—factors such as the ecological effect of animal farming and the health effect of eating animals that have been dosed with antibiotics and growth hormones.

One of the myths told about vegetarians is that they tend to be anaemic because they are deprived of the iron in meat. Accordingly, the popular perception of a vegetarian is of a weak, wan, washed out-looking individual who is deathly pale from anaemia. This is wrong. Pure vegetarians—that is, those who avoid eggs and dairy products as well as meat—are rarely anaemic. There is ample iron in the vegetables and fruit they eat. On the other hand, those vegetarians who do consume eggs and dairy products (they are sometimes referred to as lacto-ovo vegetarians) appear to be about as vulnerable to anaemia as the rest of the population. The explanation for this is that anaemia can be caused by an enzyme in milk which inhibits the body's uptake of iron. (It can also be caused by bleeding within the small intestine resulting from dairy proteins.)

We had an example of this in our own family. Our daughter, Belinda, became a vegetarian but continued to drink milk and eat cheese. During this time she suffered from anaemia. Later she moved to a pure vegetarian diet and has never been anaemic since.

There is a food revolution going on. In the United States, in May 1998, it was reported that sales of meat-substitute products had grown by 49.5 per cent during the four years 1992 to 1996. Whereas sales of these products totalled US$200 million in 1997, they were expected to soar to US$1 billion by the year 2001. The American National Restaurant Association reported that more than 50 per cent of Americans were now restricting their consumption of red meat. Because of this, some restaurant chains have begun offering veggie burgers.

Australia's vegetarian population is growing steadily, too. The likelihood is this trend will continue. Common sense demands it.

CHAPTER TEN
MIND POWER

> ***Think of something sad and your whole body tends to droop. Think of something positive, and the back straightens and the shoulders rise.***

POSSESSING THE RIGHT MENTAL ATTITUDE is an absolutely essential prerequisite if you wish to set about changing your diet. Unless you really want to do it, unless you have built the idea of better eating habits into your mental framework, you will not be able to persevere. As soon as the going gets tough, as soon as you lose that initial flush of enthusiasm, you will give up. The same is true of keeping active. The idea of being an active person—of walking regularly, or playing tennis or golf, or doing five laps of the local pool three times a week before breakfast—must be a fixture in your mind. It must colour all your thinking.

So how do you acquire the state of mind that makes it possible for you to change your lifestyle? The answer is you must develop it yourself deliberately. Sure, you may well need some outside motivation to get you going, to give you the initial momentum, but you will keep going with your new eating habits and exercise programs only if you have changed the way you think by a conscious effort.

After all, you are what you think. If you think you're old, you're old; if you think you're sick, you're sick; if you think you're unlucky, you will encounter bad luck everywhere. Every golf club has members like this. They are convinced in their own minds that they are the only golfers who ever get a bad lie, or end up behind a tree, or get a bad bounce. All the bad luck they notice is theirs and all the good luck is somebody else's.

> The one thing in life that we can control is our mind, the way we think. True, we can control what we eat and so largely control our health, but this is just a by-product of controlling our minds. If you want to change a habit, if you want to change the way you feel about something, you must change the way you think about it. If you want to give up smoking, for instance, you have to stop thinking of it as fashionable and sophisticated and think of it as filthy and unhealthy. Ultimately, the only person who can change the way you think is yourself.

I described in Chapter 9 how Judy and I became vegetarians after going on a forty-day cleansing program. Some time later an acquaintance of ours spoke to us about our new eating habits. He was so impressed by what he saw and heard that he and his wife decided to give it a try, too. So they went on the cleansing program, lasted the forty days and began following a pure vegetarian diet. I saw him about this time. In appearance he was transformed. He had lost weight and looked quite trim. For all the time I had known him he had had reddish, watery eyes. This problem had disappeared, and so had his previously blotchy complexion. All in all, he looked ten years younger.

...he was still locked into his old thought structures...he was a prisoner of his lifelong habits.

A few months later I saw him again and I could tell at once that he had reverted to his old lifestyle. His eyes were red, his waistline was protruding, his skin was as bad as ever. It transpired that he had gone back to his old eating habits after only a month. He confessed to me that it had all become too hard. He and his wife led a busy social life, and this had been disrupted repeatedly by the need to have special meals prepared for them whenever they went out. I also suspect he had come under pressure from some of his friends to give up his new, weird ideas on eating and become 'normal' again. I was disappointed for his sake. He and his wife had managed the hardest part—they had made it through the forty-day cleansing program—and then they had given up just as they were starting to reap the benefits.

Here was a case of someone who had not really changed his thinking about his lifestyle. He obviously had enough willpower to adopt a new style of eating—the fact that he and his wife had got through the forty-day cleansing showed that—but he had not made the new style of eating a part of his mental outlook. Superficially he was attracted by the idea of improving his health, but he was still locked into his old thought structures. He was a prisoner of his lifelong habits.

The loss of life's dream

We all start off with some kind of a dream. We might want to be famous, successful, powerful or maybe just wealthy. Hardly any of us achieve all we originally hoped to achieve in life. Most of us do not get even close. The realisation that we are never going to achieve the things we were striving for usually hits us in early middle age. Whether we are forty or forty-five or fifty, one day we will wake up and realise that we have gone about as far in life as we will ever go, that all those other big plans we had are never going to materialise. The horizons that once seemed to stretch endlessly into the distance close in. The dream is all but over.

The emotional effect this has on people varies with the individual. For some men, the loss of the dream can have a profound effect. I suspect it is a common cause of depression in middle-aged men. How one deals with this is necessarily a complicated matter, but the general principle that we can control how we feel by controlling how we think holds true.

Most of us face up to the reality of our lives in middle age and resign ourselves to the more limited future that seems to lie ahead. Sure, we are bound to feel some frustration at our failure to achieve the goals we set for ourselves, but what we have to guard against is allowing the frustration to affect our personalities. You can usually pick the frustrated type a mile off just by his demeanour. I never cease to be amazed at how the way we look is affected by what is going on in our minds. Think of something sad and your whole body tends to droop. Think of something positive, and the back straightens and the shoulders rise.

Can our lifestyle affect our mental state and, therefore, how we respond to the challenge of becoming middle-aged? The answer is definitely yes. The mere fact you are embarking on a campaign to improve your health and fitness has a galvanising effect on your attitude to life generally. Everyone who has tried it knows this to be true. Your old life's dream may have faded, but a new kind of dream has taken its place. Moreover, it is within your power to make sure this dream does materialise.

CHAPTER ELEVEN
AUSTRALIA'S FAT FASHION

Australian society as a whole came to accept the idea that beefiness in a male is better than slimness.

THE FASHION INDUSTRY has come in for a lot of criticism lately for using pencil-thin models to parade its clothes. Extreme thinness of the type you see on the catwalks is not normally healthy, and many young women are harming themselves physically and mentally by trying to achieve it. In other words, a false image of what the ideal female figure ought to be is making women—and teenage girls, too—aspire to an unhealthy body shape.

In my opinion, Australian men suffer from the same problem in reverse. In Australia, to be beefy is to be masculine. Conversely, it is not masculine to be slender. This is not necessarily a bad thing in itself, even though slimline men may not personally like it. The problem is the influence this image of the ideal male has had, and is having, on our eating habits. My own view is that the acceptance of body bulk as being somehow macho has encouraged Australian men to eat the kind of food that

...the average middle-aged Australian male is a stone and a half (about eight and a half kilograms) overweight

produces the bulk. Thus, the young man who lives on junk food does not feel displeased when he sees his figure broadening in the mirror. He does not think of himself as getting fat. Rather, he increasingly sees himself as beefcake.

There can be no doubt that the image has influenced our drinking habits, too. If we encounter someone in his forties or fifties at a barbeque with a big belly hanging over his shorts, most of us will take it for granted that he is a rugged, knockabout bloke. The thought will probably flash through our heads: 'What a character! I bet he's been there and done that and sunk a few beers along the way! In an instant we have made an admiring assessment of him—and all because he has a big belly!' Subconsciously, we are making several thought connections here: between heavy drinking and the macho image, between heavy drinking and his belly, between his macho image and over-eating.

The upshot of all this is that long ago Australian society as a whole came to accept the idea that beefiness in a male is better than slimness. Why should anyone be surprised, then, that the average middle-aged Australian male is a stone and a half (about eight and a half kilograms) overweight? After all, there is no social pressure on him to be slim; if anything, the social pressure has been the other way. 'He likes his beer, he loves a good feed, so he must be a good bloke!'

The gym

The gym culture which has sprung up in the past twenty years has changed this, but only to a degree. Neither the matey-boozy-beefy culture nor the gym culture offers much benefit in terms of health and genuine wellbeing. The former produces overweight men who, probably unknown to themselves, are almost certainly doomed to a rapid physical decline. The gym culture creates a minority of men who are toned and muscled but whose bodies, in most cases, have struggled under the physical strain of it all and who may well suffer for it later if they have not started to suffer already.

The truth is that only a small minority of middle-aged men are really suited, physically, to working out in a gym. The old saying 'No gain without pain' has done more harm than good, in my opinion. It has caused a lot of people to injure themselves in the quest for fitness. There is another old saying which makes a lot more sense in this regard: 'All things in moderation.' Life is not a race. We don't have to hurt ourselves in the quest for fitness.

> There is yet another saying which holds true here: 'You don't have to take your exercise seriously—just regularly.'

The conflict between eating for health and eating for pleasure is probably as old as the human race. Sixteen hundred years ago St Augustine summed up the problem in one sentence in his *Confessions*. 'What is enough for health,' he wrote, 'is not enough for pleasure.' He said he had to fight constantly against a temptation to eat too much, and he confessed that he justified his overeating in his own mind by pretending he was doing it for the sake of his health. St Augustine would have been middle-aged at the time, which might explain his interest in the subject.

How to lose weight

To slim down or even just to get rid of a paunch, you definitely don't need to pump weights in a gym. You simply need to follow the principles that have been affirmed throughout this book: eliminate as much unnecessary fat as possible from the food you eat, reduce the amount of animal protein you eat, increase the amount of fruit and vegetables you eat, and keep active, which is to say you need to walk, exercise, swim or do some other physical activity virtually every day.

> Do not fool yourself into believing that because of your physical make-up you cannot lose weight, no matter how hard you try. If you eat less or if you eat the same but eat better, you will certainly lose weight.

You often hear overweight men insisting they do not eat much, and the usual reason for this is that they are really talking about the food they eat at mealtimes. They ignore the food they eat between meals as if it did not count. If you were to look into the matter you would often find that these men eat three or four snacks a day and that the snacks they eat are fattening: ice-cream, bars of chocolate, bags of hot chips.

Snacks

These between-meal snacks were the downfall of a fellow cricketer who was well known as being overweight. His wife kept a tight rein on his eating in the home, but she could not control what he ate once he left the house. After eating the low-fat breakfast she had prepared for him, he was known to head straight for McDonald's and down a couple of hamburgers. One morning a radio reporter saw him in the street with a hamburger in each hand and broadcast the fact over the air as if it were a humorous item. Understandably, the cricketer was distressed by this. His weight was not a laughing matter for him. He had been put on a strict diet which he managed to stick to—although only at mealtimes. The bottom line was that he ate three modest meals a day plus maybe five big snacks.

Here is a second-hand anecdote from a former inmate of a Japanese prison-of-war camp, passed on to me by a friend. The former POW said he was captured in Singapore with an extremely fat Australian soldier he was friendly with, who had previously been trying without success to lose weight. The fat soldier claimed that he only ate like a sparrow yet could not lose a pound. The reality, probably, was that he ate like a sparrow at breakfast, lunch and dinner but pigged out between meals.

Once inside the Japanese camp, the weight fell off him so rapidly that after a few months his skin hung from him in folds. Some months after that, his skin tightened up, the folds disappeared and he was just another skinny POW. Happily, this soldier survived his years in the camp, although whether he put the weight back on afterwards was not reported.

If you are overweight, here is a fact which will put your excess bulk into perspective.

> The average house brick weighs about three kilograms, or a little under seven pounds. This means that if you are a stone (6.4 kilograms) overweight, you are effectively carrying about a mass of fat equal to the weight of two bricks. If you are a stone and a half overweight—which is said to be the Australian average—you are carrying three extra bricks.

The physical burden of this must be immense. Anyone who doubts this should pick up just one brick and see how heavy it is.

MEAT PLUS MILK EQUALS FAT

If you really are serious about losing weight, cut right back on the quantity of meat you eat, which is, after all, just fat and protein. It is sometimes said that you never see an obese vegetarian. This may or may not be universally true, but I have certainly not seen an obese vegetarian myself. Indeed, unless you went on an eating binge it is hard to imagine how you could be a vegetarian and be grossly overweight at the same time. There is an interesting converse to this. Many grossly overweight people on animal protein-based diets are actually undernourished, the reason being they are not getting the ninety nutrients a day they need to keep in peak health.

The other thing you need to do is cut right back on dairy foods. Fortunately, most men have long stopped drinking milkshakes by the time they reach middle age. Most continue to consume dairy foods in one form or another, though. They eat cheese and ice-cream, drink white tea and coffee, pour milk on their cereals, eat yoghurt in the belief it is a health food, cook occasionally in butter and eat any number of those packaged products, ranging from chocolates to biscuits, which contain milk derivatives. Moreover, most do it without ever thinking about the impact it is having on their health. Even if they did think about it, they would probably guess it was doing them good.

> We are the only species of animal on earth that still consumes milk products after being weaned. To make things worse, we do not even consume our own milk products but get them from another kind of animal. Dairy milk is a perfectly balanced food for calves but for nothing else. It does contain certain nutrients, but it also contains things which do us much more harm than the nutrients do us good.

The break I made with dairy foods in 1979 was final and complete. I gave up dairy milk and turned to soy or rice milk instead. I gave up dairy yoghurt and have since had nothing but soy yoghurt. I also gave up ice-cream.

As boys we were big ice-cream eaters. I remember a family gathering one Christmas at the home of one of my aunts, who wheeled in a huge

...while the benefits of avoiding red meat took awhile to become evident, the effect of giving up dairy foods was immediate.

three-tier cake made entirely of ice-cream. The top tier was the smallest and the bottom tier the biggest. We all gorged ourselves on the cake and between the lot of us we ate the top tier and half the second. Then my brothers Ian and Trevor and I settled down and ate the rest.

For a long time after giving up dairy ice-cream I ate no ice-cream at all. In recent years some quite good tofu ice-creams have come on the market, so ice-cream (only of the tofu variety, of course) again has a place on our menu from time to time. This tofu ice-cream is available at certain supermarkets, and although some of them are high in sugar they may be regarded as an occasional treat.

I gave up red meat at the same time as I gave up dairy foods, but while the benefits of avoiding red meat took awhile to become evident, the effect of giving up dairy foods was immediate. Clearly, I had been showing all the symptoms of lactose intolerance. Within days, literally, of giving up milk and cheese, these symptoms disappeared.

When calves are weaned after a few months, they no longer have any need for cow's milk. Nature has designed things this way. So why do humans drink it? Why do we eat the products made from it? It has been estimated that more than 90 per cent of the world's population is intolerant in varying degrees to lactose, the sugar in milk, which means they are subject to various digestive problems.

An even more serious problem is the allergic reaction humans have to cow's milk, often without realising the cause. The allergens in milk have been blamed for conditions such as asthma, eczema, hives, migraine, hayfever and sinusitis. Do not think you can avoid all these problems by drinking skim milk. As it happens, skim milk is rich both in allergens and in lactose.

If you are determined to lose weight, here are two reasons for cutting right back on dairy foods or eliminating them altogether. One is that they contain a lot of fat and, as we all know, fat makes you fat. The other reason is that dairy foods can inhibit the absorption of various minerals and vitamins. A deficiency of vitamins and minerals makes the body crave for more food to make up the deficiency; as a result, you instinctively eat more and so put on even more weight.

To sum up: I offer no planned diet for reducing weight. I do not need to. If you follow the basic rules of good nutrition set out in this book and if you keep active, your weight will drop whether you want it to or not.

CHAPTER TWELVE
THE PAUNCH

Somebody once likened the paunch to an iceberg—it may look big, but it is actually only the bit you see.

IF YOU ARE MIDDLE-AGED and have neglected your health for years, there is actually something to be said for being overweight, for it may well be the excess weight, rather than any decline in your general health, that finally drives you to do something about your lifestyle. Excess weight may not always be the most serious symptom of an unhealthy lifestyle, but it is certainly the most visible. It is also the one that most offends our vanity, and it would probably offend our vanity more if those of us who are overweight could see what we really look like.

This is why you sometimes hear of someone who decides to go on a crash diet after catching an unexpected glimpse of himself in a shop window, perhaps with his belly sagging over his belt buckle, and being appalled by what he sees. I have also heard of men who were motivated to get fit and healthy simply because they started to have trouble fitting into their clothes.

Which brings us to the subject of the paunch. Thankfully my body shape does not lend itself to growing a pot belly, and in any case by the time I was old enough to develop one I had begun to watch what I ate and drank. So I cannot speak of paunches with first-hand experience. But I have been surrounded by them for most of my adult life, so I do know something about them. They are, in my opinion, one of the worst things that can afflict a middle-aged man. Yet, according to one statistic that appeared recently, three out of four middle-aged men are so afflicted.

...according to one statistic that appeared recently, three out of four middle-aged men are so afflicted.

Paunches may look awful, but they must feel even worse. I strongly suspect there is a lot of self-deception involved—a point made elsewhere in this book. A friend of mine who is overweight once remarked, by way of explaining his failure to do anything about it, that he had a 'skinny mirror' at home. He was not referring to the type of 'skinny mirrors' in fashion stores which entice women to buy clothes by making them look taller and slimmer. He simply meant that the reflection he saw of himself in his mirror did not bother him. In his own eyes, when dressed in the right clothes and viewed from the right angle, he no doubt looked robustly solid—or maybe solidly robust.

> One's mental image of oneself is nearly always distorted. The image also has a habit of persisting long after the reality has disappeared.

I was small as a boy and spent my childhood thinking of myself as small.

I grew to be tall in my teens, yet even today I am not completely rid of the idea of being small. Similarly, there are many people who used to be overweight and who still think of themselves as overweight, even though they long ago slimmed down. This is said to be a cause of anorexia. The distorted self-image is one of the main reasons that overweight middle-aged men do nothing to reduce weight. They simply do not think of themselves as overweight. In their minds, they are still the slim young men of twenty or thirty years before.

THE VIEW IN THE MIRROR

So self-awareness is essential if anyone carrying a paunch is to have any hope of getting rid of it. If you are in any doubt about how you really look, get hold of a full-length mirror, strip off, stand under a bright light and look at yourself from side-on, making sure you do not pull your abdomen in. Let it all hang out and see yourself as you really are. Then, take a hand mirror and use it to look at your posterior. If you are disgusted with what you see, if you hate yourself for allowing the youthful body you once had to degenerate into its present shape, then so much the better. You will then be in a frame of mind to do something about it.

The paunch ought to be viewed with disgust, yet in certain social circles it is a badge of honour, it is proof you have lived life to the full. On the other hand, if a man has a slim figure he is regarded a little suspiciously. People wonder what he has been doing all his life—or what he has not been doing.

The hidden fat

Somebody once likened the paunch to an iceberg—it may look big, but it is actually only the bit you see, because most of the bulk is below the surface. So although a man carries a lot of fat in his paunch, you can be sure he has a lot more of it stashed away elsewhere in the body. In particular, he will have stored fat between the organs in his torso—that is, between his intestines, liver, bladder, kidneys and bowel—with the result that each of these organs will virtually be encased in fat. These organs therefore have no room to move. They are compressed on all sides, which must affect their ability to function. No wonder overweight men tend to feel sluggish!

The best people to talk to about the inside of the paunch are bowel surgeons. They will tell you that fat men are by no means their preferred patients, because having to find their way through the fat inside them makes their job much more difficult. The interesting thing is that, unlike women, men deposit relatively little fat outside the muscle wall surrounding their abdomen.

Most of the fat that forms a man's big belly, or paunch, is inside the muscle wall; that is, around and between the internal organs.

Even a man of sumo-wrestler proportions is unlikely to have a layer of fat outside the muscle wall thicker than about fifteen centimetres. Most of the fat that forms his big belly is inside the muscle wall; that is, around and between his internal organs. As any surgeon will tell you, the organs inside an overweight man with a bulging paunch are no bigger than the organs inside a slim man with a flat stomach. What causes the belly to bulge is simply the mass of fat stored inside.

One of Australia's best-known cricketers in the 1960s (who must remain nameless lest the following story causes him embarrassment) had a weight problem. He was beefy even in his playing days and put on more bulk after he retired. While in this overweight state, he developed appendicitis and had to undergo an emergency operation. The operation was successful, but the surgeon told him afterwards that it was a near thing. The former cricketer had so much fat in his abdomen that the surgeon took a long time making his way through it to reach the appendix. If the job had taken much longer, the surgeon said, the consequences might have been disastrous. As a result of this experience, not surprisingly, the former cricketer did slim down considerably.

Because of its sheer mass, a paunch can cause back problems and harm your posture. It can induce diabetes, and increases the risk of heart disease. Indeed, there is evidence to show that the fat in the abdomen is especially dangerous to the heart.

The abdominal squeeze

There is another downside. Every time you sit down, the weight of your paunch squeezes the major organs below it, especially the bowel and bladder. Over time, this may not only distort the shape of these organs but it can restrict the flow of blood to them, with possibly dire consequences. Bill Cosby probably had this in mind when he composed this prayer for middle-aged men: 'God, either give me longer arms or put my feet higher, perhaps at the knees, so I can take off my shoes without feeling I'm about to give birth.'

How to get rid of a paunch

With a few exceptions, men with paunches must lose weight. The exceptions are men with the so-called flamingo look—those who are thin everywhere except in the belly. Men with flamingo figures are usually heavy drinkers and are often alcoholics. The reason they look as they do is that the muscles in their arms, shoulders and legs have wasted away through lack of exercise while their bellies are bloated because the alcohol they drink is deposited there as fat. Such men are actually underweight because they are undernourished. They do not need to slim down, they need to cut down on their drinking or, if necessary, give it up altogether, and improve their nutrition.

In most cases, however, paunches are part of an overall weight problem. If a man's belly stands out visibly, relative to the rest of the body, it is because male hormones dictate that fat is deposited there preferentially.

If you set out to get rid of a paunch, remember that you must not merely get rid of the layer of fat around your belly but the greater mass of fat stored inside. This means it is a bigger assignment than you might have thought, but it is certainly not an impossible one. Although the belly is the first part of a man's body to build up a deposit of fat, it is also the first to lose it. This is because of the nature of the fat cells in the abdomen. They are more active metabolically.

So there is no doubt you will get rid of most of your paunch if you lose weight. Whether you can get rid of it all is debatable. According to one view, the bulge produced by a paunch can never be eliminated entirely, no matter how thin you become. You will improve your chances in this respect if you tone up your abdominal muscles by exercising. Ordinary sit-ups are effective, although I personally prefer the knee-raises described in Chapter 21.

Having succeeded in losing weight, you need to maintain a constant vigil to ensure you do not put some or all of it back on. In the process of becoming overweight we grow extra tissue; that is, we create extra cells. When we lose weight, these cells are emptied, but the cells themselves do not disappear. They are still there, waiting to be refilled with fat. This is why it is easier to put on weight after you have lost it than to put on weight in the first place.

CHAPTER THIRTEEN
THE SPORTING LIFE

> ***The trouble is that when you are twenty or thirty the ailments of advanced age seem a very long way off. Somewhere down the line, though, you will have to pay a price for ignoring your health, no matter how young you are at the moment.***

THE SEEDS OF ILL HEALTH in middle age are sown during our youth. Everyone who is middle-aged knows this, but try using it as an argument to persuade young people to change their ways and you are unlikely to make much progress. This is true even of young sportspeople—cricketers, for example.

Cricket is different from other sports. Although it is a team game, cricketers playing at the elite level tend to operate as individuals. Members of the Australian team—or any of the State teams for that matter—come together only for matches. Between times they break up, go their separate ways and have little or no contact with each other. When I played for Australia I did not always have a feeling of being part of a unit. Except on overseas tours, we did very little collectively, and in my time there was hardly any supervision of how we managed our health. Provided we turned up fit enough to play, we were left to our own devices.

We were supposed to be international sportsmen, yet, as a group, we were no more conscious of health than anyone else in the community. We ate the same kind of food that most other young Australians ate, including the mass of them who played no sport at all. A few years ago the Australian Cricket Board finally recognised the problem and appointed a nutritionist to the team. By all accounts she has done a fine job and the Australian cricketers are probably eating better as a result. Many of them, anyway. Some have proved resistant to any change. There is a story told in cricket circles of two Australian players (one of whom has since retired) who listened to a lecture from the team's nutritionist, then returned to their hotel room to get 'a real feed'. One of them phoned room service and ordered two giant hamburgers with all the trimmings, two plates of chips and two Cokes. Then, still holding the phone, he turned to the other player and said, 'And what will you have?'

Dennis Lillee was probably the most health-conscious of the Australian cricketers in my day. He had to recover from a serious back injury, and this forced him to think hard about health and fitness. I don't remember him being too choosy about the content of his diet, but he did form definite views about when and how much he should eat, based largely on his own experience. Dennis found that food slowed him up and weighed him down, and if we were bowling or about to bowl he ate virtually nothing during the day. In the evening, though, he could eat enough to feed two men. Dennis also took food supplements (I have no idea what kind of supplements they were) at a time when supplements were hardly ever heard of.

At the other end of the spectrum was my friend Doug Walters. If you wanted to profile someone who broke all the rules of good health—who smoked heavily, ate and drank badly and did hardly any training—you would need to look no further than Doug. That Walters was able to perform so brilliantly on the field over so many years is, in my view, a testimony to the capacity of the human body to prevail over adversity. Doug has not changed his habits in middle age, although I wish he would for his own sake. When we run into each other he nearly always greets me with the question: 'Are you still on that bloody diet?' My usual response is that if Doug lives beyond a certain age I will take up smoking.

THE HIGH PRICE OF UNHEALTHY LIVING

It goes without saying that people need to start looking after their health when they are young. Men who abuse their health in their twenties and thirties throw their systems off balance and so create the environment for illness to develop later. There can be no doubt that many of the illnesses and infirmities people suffer in later life, especially some of the common chronic conditions such as arthritis and adult-onset diabetes, are directly attributable to poor nutrition when they were young. The trouble is that when you are twenty or thirty the ailments of advanced age seem a very long way off. Somewhere down the line, though, you will have to pay a price for ignoring your health, no matter how young you are at the moment. If you're twenty-five years old, doing no physical exercise, eating fast food and boozing frequently, you can be sure that one day, maybe when you are in your forties or fifties or, if you are lucky, in your sixties, your body is going to cash the cheque.

This can happen in two ways, neither of them pleasant. Your body may one day demand full payment on the spot, which usually means a sudden death. You are forty-eight and living a fast life and you fall down dead of a heart attack. Or a cerebral haemorrhage gets you at fifty-four. Alternatively, your body will demand payment in instalments. Perhaps diabetes will start to afflict you at forty-seven. Or your general health will deteriorate or maybe collapse altogether, leaving you to live out the rest of your life in a state of sickness and increasing infirmity.

A family friend was a sad example of someone who was made to pay off his health debt bit by bit. He was a typical knockabout Australian who loved life, loved his beer, especially in the company of his mates in the pub, and ate whatever he felt like. All in all, he lived a jolly, hearty life. Then, in his fifties, he had a severe stroke. For nearly twenty years, until his death, he was confined to a chair, unable even to feed himself. His case was all the more pitiful because for all those years he was mentally alert and well aware of what had happened to him. I used to go around to see him. He would get

...he did not know any better then...we do know better now.

emotional because of his frustration at not being able to get up to greet me or even to speak to me properly.

The tragedy of this case, like countless others of the same type, is that the person concerned paid a terrible price for what was regarded, after all, as perfectly normal behaviour at the time. He ate, drank and generally lived his life like any other red-blooded Australian. If he was eroding his health in the process, the sad fact is he did not know any better then. We do know better today, so the same excuse cannot be used by anyone who leads this kind of life now.

While you are young you can subject your body to all kinds of poor treatment and it will seem to cope perfectly well, for the body is amazingly resilient. Beneath the surface, though, there is a lot happening. The 25-year-old who is eating a lot of junk food, binge-drinking once or twice a week and doing no exercise may still look and feel fit, but his body is already following a timetable which, unless he changes his habits, is certain to end in physical decline or worse in middle age.

Somewhere, at some time, you can be sure that abusing your health at one stage of your life will catch up on you at another stage—unless you take steps in the meantime to redeem the cheque.

The lucky people are those who get a health warning in time: a mild heart attack, perhaps, or a diagnosis of diabetes in its early stages. It is surely one of the great mysteries of human behaviour that so many people when presented with a warning of this kind choose to ignore it. It seems middle-aged men are particularly at fault in this regard. They may make the necessary changes to their lifestyle for a short while but

...the rugby team used to be fed a big steak...in the belief that this would fire them up. As we know now, it would have had exactly the opposite effect.

then slip back into the same old bad habits. Or they amend their lifestyle in some areas but not in others and so achieve little overall; for instance, the middle-aged smoker who suffers a heart attack and gives cigarettes up, yet continues to eat fatty foods and drink too much alcohol.

Attitudes to nutrition have changed. When I was growing up the conventional view was that protein was the number one energy source for athletes. Hence the view prevailing then that eating red meat made you strong and healthy. A friend who was at a boarding school in Queensland in the 1960s has told me that he and other boys in the school's first XV rugby team used to be fed a big steak on the morning of each match (steaks were otherwise never on the school's menu) in the belief that this would fire them up. As we know now, it would have had exactly the opposite effect.

Then in the 1970s carbohydrates took over from protein as the preferred energy source, and athletes and other sportspeople began filling themselves with pasta before big events. Carbohydrates came to be regarded as the high-octane fuel of the sporting world. This view has persisted ever since, although recent research has suggested that fat may also be a rich energy source for endurance athletes—distance runners, triathletes, 1500-metre swimmers and the like—and that these athletes could benefit from a high-fat diet. Whether or not this is true for them, it is obviously not true for sedentary, middle-aged men.

MENTAL ENERGY FOR CRICKET

I retired from cricket in 1984 at the age of thirty-five. Mentally, I was drained. I had lost the desire to play and succeed at the top level. Physically, though, I was capable of playing on for years. Even today, at the age of fifty, the chances are that I would physically be capable (after some fairly intensive practice in the nets) of playing a reasonable standard of cricket. What happens is that your priorities change. As a young man cricket is your only priority. Then you get married and start to have a family, and cricket becomes just one of several priorities. The family grows, the children go to school, you begin to establish business interests, and soon cricket is sliding fast down your list of priorities.

Towards the end of my cricket career I had trouble summoning up the mental energy to perform well. It gets to a stage where the fierce focus essential for playing at the top level is no longer there; you are much more easily distracted. I made a double-century against India at the Sydney Cricket Ground in 1981. Someone could have dropped a bomb in the old Showground next door that day and I would hardly have noticed it and certainly not been bothered by it. By 1984, if someone had let off a few fireworks in the Showground, I would probably have been just as interested in the fireworks as in the cricket.

Despite all this, I could certainly have struggled on and played for

...every sportsman has a finite number of playing days in him. Once he exceeds that number, regardless of how old or young he is, he is playing on borrowed time.

another three or four years. I would have been a shadow of my former self, however, and whether or not the shadow was strong or pale I would have found it all much too frustrating. The mental problem is not just about having to perform in the big matches, it is about having to do the training and the practice. If I could have just turned up to play and nothing else, I might have gone on a little longer. When my brother Ian decided to retire in 1980, I was surprised. At that stage I felt I could play cricket for the rest of my life and I thought he felt that way, too. I asked him how he could possibly give it up. He replied, 'When the day comes, you won't need anyone else to tell you; you'll know.'

He was right. When the day came, I knew. The symptoms were unmistakable. Suddenly, fielding became a drag. This surprised me, because I had always loved fielding. To play first-class cricket you must love fielding, if only because you do so much of it. Even Don Bradman spent more time fielding than he did at the batting crease. Training became a drag, too. I would come home from a hard day's work in winter and then remember I had to go for a run. To drag myself out of a chair and set off into the night suddenly became an awful chore. Without the desire, it was all becoming too hard.

The evidence suggests that every sportsman has a finite number of playing days in him. Once he exceeds that number, regardless of how old or young he is, he is playing on borrowed time. I believe I exceeded my limit twofold. Allan Border exceeded his threefold. Allan must have been receiving the same messages that we all receive when our time is drawing near, but for whatever reason—perhaps through obstinacy or perhaps because he felt he hadn't had enough—he obviously refused to listen to them.

There have been cricketers who played for Australia until much later than Allan; in fact, until well into their forties. The oldest Test player I know of was the spin bowler Bert Ironmonger. He was nearly fifty-one when he played his last Test in 1932–33, the summer of the bodyline series. Another spin bowler of about that time, Don Blackie, played Test cricket when he was nearing forty-seven.

The point that is significant about these two men, though, is that they did not start their international careers until late in life. In fact, each was forty-six on debut. What obviously kept them in the game so long was the unfulfilled ambition of playing for Australia. They still had the drive because they still had the dream. They could still maintain the desire and the focus. If Ironmonger and Blackie had managed to make the Australian team in their twenties, surely neither would have been still playing at forty.

Still, what they did was truly remarkable. Imagine starting a Test career at forty-six! Both Ironmonger and Blackie should serve as an inspiration for everyone who is middle-aged and inclined to think there is no new ground to break in life.

CHAPTER FOURTEEN
NOT A MEAT-EATER, BUT STILL A MAN

I copped a barrage of good-natured ridicule from the other golfers in the group, all of whom were big meat-eaters.

THE MAINSTREAM AUSTRALIAN culture is a meat-eating culture. Eating meat is considered a masculine thing to do. Thus, a man who does not eat meat isn't a man in the full sense of the word. Teetotallers suffer the same stigma. A man who doesn't drink is not quite a man either.

Americans seem to equate meat-eating with masculinity in much the same way. I once visited a restaurant in Orlando, Florida, with another Australian. On the menu were steaks of various sizes, ranging upwards from big, and the biggest of all was a slab of meat as broad and as thick as a telephone book. These steaks were so enormous that the restaurant offered a second steak free to anyone who could get through one. I cannot remember exactly how the offer was expressed, but it was along the lines that the second steak was a reward to anyone who was man enough to chew his way through the first. The clear implication was that you had to be a pretty tough guy, a man's man, to eat all that meat. At the table next to us were four Texans who were silly enough to do it. Out came the second round of huge steaks, and by the time we left the restaurant the Texans were still working their way through these.

I do not mind being regarded as somehow different or even a little odd because I am a vegetarian. If I do get exasperated occasionally with remarks that are made to me about it, it is because they stem from ignorance. My attitude to the people who make these remarks is: 'Think what you like about vegetarians, but at least give me the credit for making a reasoned choice based on personal experience and careful evaluation. I tried both ways, the meat-eating and the vegetarian, and I have chosen the latter. Until you try both, you are hardly entitled to criticise me for that.'

My brother Ian never ceases to rib me about being a vegetarian, and being an older brother perhaps he has a right to do so. For a couple of cricket seasons he and I worked together in the Channel Nine commentary team, which meant that the two of us flew repeatedly about the country on the same routes and at around the same time. I always prebooked a vegetarian meal on the plane, and to my amusement the airline sometimes mixed up our initials and served Ian the vegetarian meal instead. I heard it irritated him, which amused me. It was a kind of revenge.

Some of the best vegetarian food I have tasted has been at the homes of people who have never before prepared a vegetarian meal.

Ian may not be a vegetarian, but he is

People tend to have strange ideas about what constitutes a vegetarian meal.

certainly careful about what he eats and he does look after his health generally. For a man now moving through his mid-fifties, he is extremely fit.

It would be silly to pretend that the life of a pure vegetarian does not have its complications. The most common problem, and probably the most difficult to deal with, is the one that arises when you are invited to someone's place for a meal. When this happens, there are basically three possibilities. You can eat before you go (hardly conducive to a good dinner-party atmosphere). You can take your own food with you (an embarrassing option for all concerned). Or you can put your host to the trouble of preparing vegetarian food specially for you.

The difficulty this last possibility presents should not be underestimated. As every vegetarian would know from experience, the prospect of having to feed a couple of vegetarians actually freaks a lot of people out. The way many people deal with it is by striking you off their list of dinner guests. So being a vegetarian can affect your social life and, in a sense, marginalise you.

On the other hand, some of the best vegetarian food I have tasted has been at the homes of people who have never before prepared a vegetarian meal but who have made an enormous effort to ensure that the meal they prepared for me was top-class. On occasions like this, I feel grateful to the point of embarrassment.

'Almost a vegetarian'

Curiously, there are many people who in their own minds are only a step away from being vegetarians but who actually eat a lot more meat than they realise. If I reply to a dinner invitation by saying, as I usually do, 'I'm more than happy to come, but the problem is I'm a strict vegetarian and I don't want to put you to any trouble,' many people will say, 'No trouble at all. We're almost vegetarians ourselves.' I could not count the number of people I have heard describe themselves as 'almost vegetarians'.

In fact, some of these people have an appetite for meat that Conan the Barbarian would be proud of, yet still think of themselves as 'almost vegetarians'. Others turn out to be people who, to their credit, do eat a lot of vegetables and fruit but who nevertheless base a majority of their meals on meat. Perhaps because the lump of meat on the plate looks small by comparison with the vegetables surrounding it, they imagine it is almost a vegetarian meal. This simply shows a lack of understanding of what it means to be a vegetarian.

The kind of people I have just described no doubt think they are following a balanced diet; that is, a diet that is balanced between meat and vegetables. It is wishful thinking, because a properly balanced diet is nothing of the kind. How could it be, when they are consuming three times more protein than they need?

I have noticed another curious reaction from people who invite me to eat with them knowing I am a vegetarian. Often I detect unease on their part, as if they are afraid I will be judging them by their eating habits. I sense they feel embarrassed, even a little guilty, to be doing something (in this case, eating meat) which I refrain from doing myself. So during the meal they will make comments such as, 'Of course, we don't eat much meat,' by way of apologising for themselves. The truth is I do not care what other people eat. It is none of my business. If someone asks me, I am happy to talk to him or her about the health advantages of a vegetarian diet, but I certainly do not go around preaching to people. God spare us from self-righteous vegetarians!

On the vegetarian's side, there are problems, too. A common one is having to remember you are different. If you are asked to a function, you have to let the people inviting you know that they need to have a vegetarian meal ready. I can still forget to do this. I will be setting off to speak at a dinner somewhere and suddenly realise as I walk out the door that I neglected to mention I am a vegetarian. Then I have to make a last-minute call. If the function is at an international-class hotel, there is rarely a problem. Big hotels are always able to come up with a vegetarian meal at short notice. If the function is at, say, a businessmen's club, a last-minute call to say you are a vegetarian can throw everyone into a panic. I know, because I've had to do it several times.

People tend to have strange ideas about what constitutes a vegetarian meal. At quite a few of the official luncheons and dinners I have attended in the past few years I have found a plate of steamed vegetables awaiting me. Steamed vegetables on their own are a pretty unappetising dish, although I am not complaining about that. The point I find interesting is that the well-meaning people who serve the steamed vegetables apparently believe this is what vegetarians like to eat. This sort of ignorance is everywhere.

First trial of a new lifestyle

Within weeks of becoming a vegetarian I had my first testing experience of being an odd one out. I was one of a group of golfers from the Royal Canberra club who went to Melbourne for a golfing week. We stayed and played at the Victoria Golf Club. Realising the fuss I might cause if I turned up unannounced, I phoned ahead and spoke to the catering manager there, who assured me they would have no trouble providing me with vegetarian meals. She asked me to send her some recipes of the type of meals—breakfast, lunch and dinner—I would like. I did this, and the club obviously went to some trouble to obtain what was needed.

During my week there, I was taken into the kitchen and shown an area in the pantry that the chef had reserved for my special needs. There, on a shelf, was coconut milk, soy milk, soy sauce, tofu and the various other special ingredients. I felt embarrassed and apologised to the chef for causing him so much bother. He said it was no bother at all. In fact, he enjoyed the challenge of preparing food that was different from the same old meals that he turned out week after week.

I was revved up with so much energy that I could have gone around the course again.

For the first few days I copped a barrage of

good-natured ridicule from the other golfers in the group, all of whom were big meat-eaters. 'What kind of rabbit food are we having tonight?' 'Sure I can't tempt you with a steak?' 'I hope the smell of my bacon and eggs doesn't bother you.' This went on for several days. It was no more than I expected, so I did not mind it. Nor did I feel under any pressure to revert to my old eating habits.

Around the middle of the week something interesting happened. Their attitude changed. Suddenly, they were looking at my plate and asking: 'What's that you've got there. I wouldn't have minded some of that.' They could see that the meals I was eating were more interesting and looked tastier than theirs. Probably they also noticed that I had a lot more energy than I had ever had before. Most of them had known me for some time, so they were able to tell the difference.

We played eighteen holes each morning and then broke for lunch in the clubhouse. The others ate their normal heavy, meat-based meals, which invariably included a pile of hot chips. I ate nothing but soup. After another nine holes in the afternoon the others would call it quits for the day and collapse in a chair, while I was revved up with so much energy that I could have gone around the course again.

I found that trip very useful because it enabled me to compare myself directly with men of my own age who were eating the food I had eaten before. In a perverse sort of way, the trip confirmed for me that by becoming a vegetarian I had made the right decision.

CHAPTER FIFTEEN
Mealtime at the Chappells'

Having eaten both styles of food, I am able to say as a statement of fact that the meat-based food which most ordinary Australians eat is both more limited in scope and more mundane than vegetarian food.

I AM A *PURE* VEGETARIAN. With one exception, all the foods I eat are of plant origin. The exception is honey, which I still eat and which is known to be beneficial to health. There are other pure vegetarians commonly known as vegans, who go one step further. They avoid all animal products not only in their diets but in all areas of their lives. Vegans do not eat honey, for instance, and they avoid using leather goods and even woollen goods.

Vegetarians find that the hardest point to get across to meat-eaters about vegetarian food is the enormous variety of it. For the majority of (non-vegetarian) Australians, meat is the centrepiece of nearly every meal and the vegetables that surround the meat seem to them to be no more than a bland and uninteresting accompaniment. When these

...there are dishes I used to enjoy that I now eat in vegetarian form...burgers, shepherd's pie and curries.

people think of vegetarians, they imagine this is the kind of food they eat: steamed or baked vegetables, salads, boiled rice and the like. All very wholesome no doubt, but very boring and all but tasteless.

Having eaten both styles of food, I am able to say as a statement of fact that the meat-based food which most ordinary Australians eat is both more limited in scope and more mundane than vegetarian food. Most meat-eating families get by on about a half-dozen standard meals (casseroles, chops, shepherd's pie, roast lamb, mince and pasta etc), which they eat in endless rotation. The ordinary vegetarian household (like the Chappells') regularly chooses from a much more varied menu.

FRESH FLAVOURS

What do I personally like eating? Well, curries are now a big favourite of mine. Anyone who has eaten a vegetarian curry in India will understand why. In India, they make many of their curries mild. Sure, they put chillies and other hot spices on side-plates in case you wish to fire up the meal, but they do not make hot curries as a matter of course as some restaurants unfortunately do in Australia. Because the curries are mild, they allow you to taste the flavours, which is why I prefer mild curries myself.

I discovered all this for the first time when the Indian cricketer Bishen Bedi invited a few of us to dinner at his home one summer when he was playing county cricket for Northamptonshire. Bish's wife had prepared a traditional Indian curry, and the curry itself turned out to be surprisingly mild. Ian loved hot curries, and I could see he felt a little let down, for we had both expected a curry hot enough to set out mouths on fire. Indians also tend to offer a variety of curries, instead of slapping a big helping of one curry on your plate in the Western manner, and this is a practice we have come to follow.

I love pasta dishes. I love Asian-style dishes in general and rice dishes in particular. I love vegetarian-style laksas.

Tofu has naturally become an important part of the food I eat. At some vegetarian restaurants you can order a mock-meat dish made of tofu which is so like the real thing I would defy anyone wearing a blindfold to tell the difference. Replicating the taste of the meat dishes is not really so difficult. When you eat a meal of sweet and sour pork, for instance, what you are really tasting is the sweet and sour sauce. Replace the pork with tofu and it tastes much the same.

At some eating places you could not tell the difference even if you took off the blindfold. I know of one or two Chinese vegetarian restaurants in Sydney that serve a vegetarian version of, say, sweet and sour pork or chicken chow mein which, in appearance as well as taste, is an exact replica of what it pretends to be. At one of these restaurants I noticed that the 'fish' even had the indentations that are normally left when the bones are filleted out. I asked the people at the restaurant how on earth they did it. They told me they cook the tofu in layers with sheets of a seaweed, nori, interspersed between them. The nori leaves an imprint which looks exactly like fish bones.

The pleasure of meat-less meals

It is impossible to believe that any vegetarian who eats good vegetarian food could ever crave the taste of a meat dish. Vegetarian meals simply have more natural flavours. At the same time, there are certain meat dishes I used to enjoy which I now eat in vegetarian form. In my meat-eating days I used to love burgers, and I still love a tofu burger or some type of vegetarian burger, which tastes almost the same as meat burgers, only better.

Shepherd's pie is another example. It used to be one of my favourite meals. We now eat an equally tasty vegetarian equivalent of it, with the usual potato on top and a lentil pie beneath. For those who would like to give it a try, instructions on how to prepare it are in the recipe section on page 214.

If you like Chinese food and would like to experience it vegetarian style, you could do no better than having a yum cha lunch at one of the Chinese vegetarian restaurants. This will allow you to sample various dishes and so expose you to a whole range of vegetarian food at one sitting.

Anyone thinking of eating vegetarian food would be advised to dine out at a good vegetarian restaurant.

Good vegetarian food

Anyone thinking of eating vegetarian food would be advised to dine out at a good vegetarian restaurant, for this will dispel forever the notion that vegetarian food is no more than rabbit food. Unfortunately, many vegetarian restaurants in Australia are extremely frugal in style and decor. The food may be great, but you have to eat it on bare tables in spartan surroundings. This is a pity, because it tends to perpetuate the idea that all vegetarians are alternative-lifestyle people. There is one restaurant in Sydney which is not like this, or at least wasn't like it when I was last there. It is in Rozelle and is called the **Harvest**. The owners have another outstanding restaurant in Jersey Road, Woollahra. Sydney has other fine vegetarian restaurants. One is **Laurie's** in Burton Street, Darlinghurst. It has an excellent takeaway section, and my personal favourite there is a tofu burger with a mild chilli sauce. Two others which have impressed me are **Bodhi** in Hay Street in the city and **Vegal Kitchen** in Frenchmans Road, Randwick.

There are similar restaurants in other cities which I can recommend to mainstream people who are curious to know what good vegetarian food tastes like. In Melbourne try the **Vegetarian Adventure** in Nicholson Street, Carlton North, or the **Shakahari** in Lygon Street, Carlton; in Adelaide the **Moonbright** Chinese restaurant, formerly known as **Blossoms**, in Hindley Street in the city, or the **Green Olive** in Hutt Street; in Canberra **Bernadette's** in Wakefield Gardens, Ainslee, or **Erewan Thai** in Botany Street, Phillip; and in Perth the **Esplanade** and the **Happy**

Buddha, both in the city, and **Peppers Vegetable Eating House** in Beaufort Street, Mt Lawley. In Brisbane I have no hesitation in recommending a restaurant in Enoggerra Road, Newmarket, called **Squirrels**. It is my favourite restaurant in Australia. Indeed, I would rate it the best of all the vegetarian restaurants I have eaten at, anywhere in the world.

CHAPTER SIXTEEN
FITTING IN WITH THE FAMILY

> ***I find it hard to imagine how any married man, especially one with a family, could hope to adopt a new style of eating if he did not have his wife on side.***

A MARRIED MAN DOES NOT need his family's support to get fit. He can do it on his own. He can climb out of bed in the morning without disturbing his wife and do his daily exercises. Or he can leave the family sitting in front of the television after dinner and set off on his own for his regular evening walk. It is not nearly so easy for him, though, to change his eating habits on his own. At the least, he will need his wife's moral support for what he is doing, regardless of whether or not she does most of the cooking. I find it hard to imagine how any married man, especially one with a family, could hope to adopt a new style of eating if he did not have his wife on side.

So obtaining your wife's blessing is essential, in my opinion, before you make any move to change your eating habits. My guess is that most wives in this situation would be willing to provide at least passive support, despite the inconvenience and occasional irritation it may cause

...it would be a mistake (possibly a fatal one!) to underestimate the disruption you can cause to the family's normal kitchen routine when you set out to change your eating habits.

them, for most would surely wish to have a healthier husband with a fitter, trimmer body. Tell your wife that you intend getting rid of your pot belly, and she will probably cheer you on.

Yet it would be a mistake (possibly a fatal one!) to underestimate the disruption you can cause to the family's normal kitchen routine when you set out to change your eating habits. Essentially, two meals have to be prepared at each sitting, one for you and one for the rest of the family. This is a big ask if your wife does most of the cooking, so it is a matter you need to approach with tact.

Obviously, the first thing to do is convince your wife of the health benefits you stand to gain from eating more nutritious food. In other words, she needs to know that you are not merely indulging a whim by switching to a different style of food. She needs to know you are doing it as a means to an end, the end in this case being a marked improvement in your health and a prolongment of your active life.

If you have approached your wife with tact and she is still unwilling to cooperate with your new eating plans, how do you get on then? Frankly, this is not an easy question to answer. I know of a few men who were keen to change their eating habits but abandoned the idea because of resistance from their wives. So it is no small problem. Of course you could always offer to do the extra cooking and meal preparation yourself. But this is often impracticable, and if your wife does most of the cooking she probably does not want you cluttering the kitchen, anyway. One possibility is to persuade your wife to give it a fortnight's trial. Promise her that if making separate meals proves too big a hassle you will give it all up—and then try to ensure it doesn't prove too big a hassle.

Adjustable meals

A better solution, though, because it minimises disruption in the kitchen, is to eat variations of the meals the rest of the family is eating rather than entirely different meals. Certain dishes lend themselves to this. For instance, you could choose to have a vegetable curry while the rest of the family is having a meat-based curry. You would all be eating the same rice, the same vegetables, the same curry sauce and the same extras (banana, tomato, cucumber, nuts and so on). The only difference would be that your serving of curry would have been cooked in a separate pan and would be minus the meat.

You can do the same with spaghetti bolognaise; in other words, use the same sauce and just prepare one serving without meat. Or do it with a casserole. In this case you cook only one meal and simply remove the meat from your own serving. This leaves the meat-based juice, gravy and a degree of fat behind, so it is not a vegetarian meal, but it does contain a lot less protein and fat than the other servings on the table which include the meat.

Burgers are perhaps the simplest of all these adjustable meals. Make them exactly the same for everyone—that is with buns or toasted bread, salad and sauce—except that the rest of the family gets meat patties and you get non-meat patties. The latter are sold in most supermarkets and are made variously from soy, grains, nuts and the like. They look the same as the normal meat burger, they have the same texture and they taste the same—only better. Alternatively, simply char-grill a piece of tofu instead of the meat.

If you need to find a replacement for eggs, remember that mashed potato or fresh breadcrumbs (that is, not from a packet) plus a little lemon juice can bind ingredients like herbs, sea salt, cracked pepper with lentils, mashed chickpeas or lightly cooked mashed vegetables.

> Here is a tip for the true believers. Never throw away any liquids from cooked grains, pulses or vegetables. Store the liquid in a glass container in the fridge and, when needed, warm up small amounts throughout the day, adding one teaspoonful of soya sauce and/or one teaspoonful of honey. It makes a very nourishing drink and you'll be getting all the plant hormones so important to your nutrition.

Learn but don't lecture

A Sydney woman whose husband has been eating different meals from the rest of the family in an attempt to improve his nutrition spoke to me after she heard I was writing this book. 'It's one thing for a husband to feel good about the healthy food he is eating,' she said. 'It's another for him to make remarks about the food the rest of us are eating. Please tell all the husbands who read your book to keep their comments to themselves at the table.' It transpired that this woman's husband had kept criticising the food she and the children were eating—while they were eating it—saying it was unhealthy and filling their arteries with fat.

Do your own thing and say nothing—unless, of course, you are asked why you eat the kind of food you eat.

All of us would sympathise with her. Not only within the family but in all the circles you mix in, it is a mistake ever to adopt a superior tone when talking about the food you eat. There is nothing other people dislike more. Much better to just do your own thing and say nothing—unless, of course, you are asked why you eat the kind of food you eat. Then, by all means, spread the word.

The ideal situation is one in which you and your wife embark on the change of lifestyle together. This is what Judy and I did, of course. When it comes to preparing meals the advantages are obvious. The other advantage, especially in the first few weeks, is that you can motivate each other and make sure you each stick to your eating and exercising plan.

When Judy and I decided to remain vegetarians, we were careful not to attempt to coerce our three children into joining us; however, the fact that we had changed our diet naturally impacted on their lives, too. The one who was most vocal in opposition was our daughter, Belinda. She made it clear she thought the whole thing absurd. That was in 1993. Belinda's thinking has changed. Today, she is a pure vegetarian. Our older son, Stephen, has made substantial modifications to his eating habits. Most of the meals he prepares for himself are pure vegetarian. Our youngest, Jonathan, is a dedicated meat-eater, but we try to ensure that he has enough fruit and salad, and we provide him with excellent vitamin and mineral supplements.

CHAPTER SEVENTEEN
THE HEALTH ALTERNATIVE

I am much happier knowing that I am responsible for ensuring I maintain good health—that my health and wellbeing are not at the mercy of someone, or something, else.

IF YOU WERE TO SURVEY every man aged between forty and seventy in Australia, you would find that a majority of them, perhaps nearly all of them, would like to be healthier and fitter than they are. The trouble is they don't know where to start. For most men, the only point of reference in matters of health is their doctor. But if they go to their doctor, the chances are the doctor will be more concerned about relieving their ailments than improving their overall health. You cannot blame the doctors for that. The training they do prepares them better for prescribing drugs than for giving advice on nutrition. My impression is that most doctors know little more about nutrition than anyone else. I must also observe, on the basis of personal experience, that there is a reasonable chance your own doctor is overweight and physically unfit. He or she may even be a smoker. Again, you cannot condemn the doctor for

There are many things you can do on your own, and you need to be prepared to take the responsibility for finding out what they are.

that, but nor can you blame the patient for feeling less than confident in the treatment being offered.

For the past fifty years at least the practice of medicine—at least at the GP level—has been largely a treatment of symptoms. People go to doctors with a specific symptom, and as a general rule the doctors prescribe a drug (more often than not an antibiotic) to treat that symptom. Rarely do they try to analyse a patient's lifestyle to find the underlying cause of the symptoms, notwithstanding the abundance of evidence to show that most complaints can be traced back to some lifestyle factor. Again, it is hard to blame the doctors for this. Because of the way modern medical practice is structured, the time doctors have available for each patient does not allow them, even if they wanted to, to investigate what their patients have been eating and drinking, whether they have been obtaining all the necessary minerals and other nutrients, how much they have been exercising, and so on.

People reading this book at least need to be aware that there is another option. You may need to see a doctor, of course, and the doctor may need to prescribe you drugs, but you should realise there is an alternative, that there are other, more natural, ways in which you can improve your health and your mobility. There are many things you can do on your own, and you need to be prepared to take the responsibility for finding out what they are.

There is an alternative health system operating successfully in Australia, but for the majority of Australians who have never had any contact with it the system is not always easy to tap into. For instance, there is a small but growing number of doctors, mainly GPs, who practise holistic medicine. I refer here to those doctors who prefer to prescribe drugs as a last option, not as a first—doctors who are prepared to deal with each patient's symptoms not in isolation but, rather, in the context of his or her overall health.

How do you go about finding such a doctor? One way is to contact the Australasian College of Nutritional and Environmental Medicine in Melbourne. The college maintains a register of GPs who have trained at the college and who practise holistic medicine. Many of them use herbal and homoeopathic medicine. Typically, they place the onus of healing on the patients themselves, not on pills in a bottle. At last report, there were more than 200 doctors of this kind on the register in Australia. You can find out the name and location of the one nearest to you by phoning the college on (03) 95896088. The college also has an informative web site (www.acnem.org).

Then there are the naturopaths. One possibility, if you want to be personally recommended to a naturopath, is to inquire at your local health food store. Indeed, health food shops are usually good contact points for alternative health practitioners of all types. Many have noticeboards in the window providing details of local naturopaths. Some stores also have 'resident' practitioners— that is, naturopaths who are available for consultations in the stores at certain times of the week. Otherwise, the simplest thing to do is consult the Yellow Pages. In the

Sydney Yellow Pages, for instance, the listings of naturopaths extend over almost four full pages.

Middle-aged men who have never been to a naturopath before may well feel hesitant about making their first visit. No doubt they are fearful of ending up in the clutches of a quack. This is completely understandable, but if you choose a naturopath who belongs to a well-known, professional organisation you can be as sure as it is possible to be that you are in responsible hands. They are likely to be well-trained and well-credentialled. Turn again to the Yellow Pages. The naturopaths who belong to these professional organisations are listed clearly.

Here is a question that is likely to arise if you start thinking of visiting a natural health practitioner: should you go to a GP who is practising holistic medicine or to a naturopath? I am loath to recommend either group in preference to the other, for both provide an excellent service. Indeed, you will often find these GPs working in conjunction with naturopaths in the same clinic. After examining a patient the GP may call in the naturopath to plan a nutritional program. The GPs do offer a couple of advantages, however, which ought to be mentioned here. One is that they have access to the full range of drugs—and do not forget that treatment by drugs can be necessary and sometimes life-saving. The other is that if you see a GP you are eligible for the Medicare rebate.

GPs who use the holistic approach do not see themselves as practising 'alternative medicine'.

As I write this, there is a campaign under way to get the Australian Government to introduce controls on the sale of vitamins and minerals. This ought to be resisted at all costs, for it would severely restrict the freedom of people to make use of alternative health options. It would probably make vitamins, minerals and other alternative medicines less accessible to the public and more expensive.

Healing: the patient's responsibility

The point was made before that GPs of the holistic school put the onus of healing squarely on the shoulders of the patient. It is up to the patients themselves to make the lifestyle and dietary changes necessary to rectify the imbalance existing in their systems and so fix each of their ailments at its origin. Personally, I find this concept extremely appealing. I am much happier knowing that I am responsible for ensuring I maintain good health—that my health and wellbeing are not at the mercy of some-one, or something, else. Once you take on this responsibility, you will probably find it adds another dimension to your life. The subject of health and nutrition becomes an absorbing interest, a kind of hobby. This is especially so if you are middle-aged.

There is plenty of evidence to show that many of the ailments that beset us in middle age, which have always been blamed on wear and tear and the ageing process, are more often than not the result of poor nutri-tion. Arthritis is one of these. I suffered from it myself during and after my playing days. I had it in my left ankle, in the big toe of my right foot and in my fingers. I did not see a doctor about it because I knew there was nothing doctors could do to fix the problem. They would prescribe drugs to relieve the pain but that was all. Taking drugs was the last thing I wanted to do, so instead I wore a copper arthritis bangle, which did seem to ease the discomfort. By the early 1990s I was resigned to the idea of being an arthritis sufferer for the rest of my life. All I could hope for was that the condition did not worsen. Then in 1993 I became a pure vegetarian. Not long after this, almost without my realising it, the symptoms began to fade. They have now disappeared altogether. I have been 'cured' of arthritis by changing my eating habits.

> Even when poor nutrition does not appear to be the root cause of an illness, good nutrition may still provide the solution. The move towards 'natural therapies'—that is, treating illnesses by changing your diet and taking nutritional medicines and herbs —has been one of the most interesting developments in international medicine in recent years.

Even cancers are now being treated in this way. Prostate cancer, which appears in 15 per cent of Australian men before they die, is one of these. Anyone wishing to look into natural treatments for prostate diseases, including cancer, may well be interested in an article on the subject written by the Sydney doctor Emmanuel Veripatis, which appeared in the autumn 1998 edition of *New Vegetarian and Natural Health* magazine.

GPs who use the holistic approach do not see themselves as practising 'alternative medicine'. They prefer to say they are practising 'complementary' medicine. In other words, the service they offer is meant to be in addition to, not instead of, orthodox medicine. This may be true, but all the signs suggest that the holistic method of treatment is where the practice of medicine is heading—that over the next ten years we can expect to see a marked change in the way doctors treat their patients.

Not long ago I was checked out by a Sydney doctor who uses the holistic approach. She made this same point: that before long doctors as a whole will feel compelled by market forces to start practising holistic medicine, whether they want to or not. The interesting thing is that the pressure for them to do so is coming not from above but from below. It is public demand that is forcing the change. There is a groundswell movement getting under way. People are becoming increasingly dissatisfied and disillusioned with orthodox medicine. They want to prevent health problems occurring rather than to wait until they do occur and then hope to get them treated.

Occasionally, it is nice to be in the vanguard.

CHAPTER EIGHTEEN
INACTIVITY: A MIDDLE-AGE MINDSET

...if you approach middle age with the idea that is a time of opportunity, you are sure to enjoy it and will probably find it particularly productive.

PEOPLE BECOME MIDDLE-AGED in the mind as well as the body. Once someone starts to think 'I can't do that' or 'I shouldn't do that' he is on his way to becoming mentally middle-aged. Without doubt, the mental side of the equation is as important as the physical. Once you start even thinking that you can't do something, it will not be long before you won't physically be able to do it.

In a sense, middle age is not in itself a problem. The problem is surrendering to the physical decline that people traditionally associate with middle age. There is a general acceptance that beyond the age of forty your body starts to run down like an old car. People take it for granted that in middle age they will become less and less active, that they will have to go to the doctor more often, that they will suffer from all kinds of pains and minor disabilities that they did not have before.

Attitude is everything. If you have the idea when you reach forty-five or fifty you enter a twilight zone where the sun is setting, you are half-finished already. But if you approach middle age with the idea that is a time of opportunity, you are sure to enjoy it and will probably find it particularly productive. Just the other day I saw the fashion guru Giorgio Armani quoted as saying on his sixtieth birthday that he was enjoying the most productive and enjoyable period of his life. Armani is a middle-aged man with the right attitude to middle age.

I have a special admiration for those middle-aged people we meet or hear about who have struck out in new directions.

In my own case, I consciously approached middle age as a time when, free from previous encumbrances, I would be able to enter new fields, attempt new ventures and generally make some changes in my life. I saw it as a time of challenge. This is how it has turned out. In my mid- to late-forties, I sold out of several businesses that had been a big part of my life for many years. I moved home from Brisbane to Canberra and more recently to Adelaide. I chanced my arm in a couple of ventures that were entirely new to me. And, of course, I changed my eating habits and, with them, my lifestyle.

There was a temptation to stay in the comfort zone and just coast along, without trying anything new. I am pleased now I resisted it. I have a special admiration for those middle-aged people we meet or hear about who have struck out in new directions. Winston Churchill was one. He was hardly a picture of robust health, but he did have the right attitude to middle age. In the 1920s, when he was over fifty years old, he took up bricklaying, having signed on as an adult apprentice of the bricklayers' union. He built a summer house and high garden walls, which you can still see if you visit his country home, Chartwell.

Whether or not Churchill had much physical energy, he certainly had plenty of mental energy. In fact, the two usually go hand in hand. Energy is one commodity we do not have to lose as we move through middle age. My own energy levels were quite low in my twenties, and they started to rise only after I changed my eating habits. Today, having passed fifty, I certainly have more energy than I had twenty-five years ago; not the kind of energy you need for a ten-kilometre run, of course, but the energy you need to do the ordinary, day-to-day activities that fill our lives. This is the kind of energy that we all need to have.

Recently I was asked by a journalist to define middle age. I replied it was that time of life when, instead of putting your beer down and jumping out of your chair to join your mates when they start kicking a football outside, you say to yourself, no, bugger it. I think I'll stay where I am.

THE IMPORTANCE OF MENTAL IMAGE

I was joking, of course, but there was truth in what I said. There comes a time in life when you feel like staying in the chair and when you are entitled to stay in the chair. But you cannot, must not, stay in the chair indefinitely. It is vital that you maintain a mental image of yourself as an active person. In a sense, maintaining this image of yourself is just as important as actually being active. If you think of yourself as an active person you will stay active. Conversely, if you start thinking of yourself as a couch potato, a couch potato is certainly what you will become. If you are convinced you have reached an age at which aches and stiffness are inevitable, you can be sure your body will ache and your joints feel stiff.

...when the day comes that he wants to kick the football he ought to be physically capable of doing it.

The importance of self-image for the middle-aged man cannot be overstressed. Everyone reading this will be able to think of someone who is not so old in years but decidedly old in mind and in manner. You can see them walking about the streets any day of the week—younger men who stand, move about and generally conduct themselves like older men. Even their faces wear aged, worn-out expressions.

On the other hand, we can all think of men of the opposite type: men brimming with vitality who might be in their seventies but move and speak as decisively as someone twenty years younger. If you could look into their heads I am sure you would find that in every case these men genuinely think of themselves as robust and energetic. That is the key to it.

The onset of middle-age decline is an interesting subject for study. Does the body weaken first and the mind then make the necessary adjustment? In other words, when you no longer feel like jumping out of the chair to run about and kick a football, is the mind simply protecting the body, which it realises is no longer up to such a hectic activity? Or does middle age originate in the mind? Do you lose the will, the spirit, to be active before you lose the physical ability to be active?

A CHICKEN-AND-EGG ARGUMENT

It is a chicken-and-egg argument which may never be settled, but my personal view is that middle age usually begins as a state of mind. That said, it is obvious that your state of mind is affected by your physical condition, which in turn largely depends on your eating habits. It would be silly, though, to try to maintain a youthful state of mind indefinitely in the hope of remaining youthfully fit and vigorous. Your state of mind must change. Mine has certainly changed. I have tried hard over the years to remain physically capable, yet I often find myself, when offered the chance of joining in some physical activity that I used to enjoy, deciding that it is not for me. This is only natural.

Consider again the case of the fellow who decides to stay in his chair instead of kicking the football. If he is over forty, he is perfectly entitled to stay in the chair if this happens to be his preference on that particular day. The important thing—and here I am reinforcing a point made elsewhere in this book—is that when the day comes that he wants to kick the football he ought to be physically capable of doing it. I believe this ought to be an objective of every middle-aged man. Throughout our forties, fifties, sixties and beyond we ought to be able to exert ourselves physically when we want to—to climb onto the roof to clear the gutters or maybe play a vigorous game of ping pong—without the fear of feeling stiff, sore and sorry for days afterwards.

Do you lose the will, the spirit, to be active before you lose the physical ability to be active?

I had a personal example of this not long ago. It happened that several members of my younger son's A-grade baseball team in Canberra went off to play in the national championships, which left the team short of a couple of players. When it seemed the team would have to forfeit the match, I suggested to one of the other fathers, who, like me, had played baseball in his youth, that we should fill the gap. The problem was we had no pitcher, so I volunteered to do the job. We played, and I pitched nine innings in the game. I took a hiding, but it was great fun. Indeed, I had forgotten just how much fun you can have doing something as simple as running about and throwing and hitting a ball.

I was forty-eight years old at the time. For a few weeks before the game I prepared myself for the pitching with some light throwing practice. But I had not pitched, as such, in thirty years, and nine innings is a lot of pitching for anyone of any age. For the last two or three innings I struggled, but I made it through, and afterwards I went for a run and did some stretching exercises.

The big test was how I pulled up over the next few days. Well, I woke next morning and felt fine. This was encouraging, but it is usually on the second day that aches and stiffness are worst. The second day came and I still felt fine. My throwing arm and shoulder were not sore at all; nor were my back and legs. Strangely, I ached in only one place, my left buttock, and this was obviously because I had thrown all my weight over my left leg each time I pitched.

I was pleasantly surprised at how well I had weathered it all. I felt pleased with myself. I had done hardly any running in the previous ten years, but I'd kept active during this time with both a daily exercise program and a walking program, which I had stuck to faithfully. In particular, I had done a lot of stretching. All this, it now seemed, had paid off. Playing baseball that day wasn't something I had planned to do. It isn't something I may necessarily want to do again. The point is, though, that when the need arose, when I wanted to do it, I was able to do it.

DID YOU EVER SEE YOUR FATHER RUN?

A friend about my own age once made an interesting observation to me. He said he did not ever see his father run, and he speculated this was because men of his father's generation considered it somehow undignified to break out of a walk once they passed, say, forty. I could not say this about my own father. As a boy I used to watch him play grade cricket in Adelaide when he must have been about forty years old. After that, though, I cannot remember him ever going faster than a walk.

It was the same with my grandfather on my mother's side, Vic Richardson. Vic had been a great all-round sportsman and by all accounts a very active man in his day, full of vigour and vitality. I have memories of him going back to the time he was about sixty, and among them is a vague recollection of him playing tennis at some time. Otherwise, I do not remember him exerting himself in physical activity.

There may be some truth in my friend's observation. I think middle-aged men of previous generations did regard running as somehow beneath them. I strongly suspect this was because of the middle-age mindset I referred to earlier; that is, the acceptance of middle age as a period of physical decline. Middle-aged men did not run because, consciously or sub-consciously, they thought they were past it. Running was something boys and young men did.

Middle-aged men did not run because, consciously or sub-consciously, they thought they were past it.

Happily, this idea changed long ago. For twenty-five years now middle-aged joggers have been a familiar sight. (In fact, for reasons I will discuss in Chapter 20, they would really be better off walking than jogging.) In other ways, though, that middle-age mindset has not changed.

My previous assertion that middle age ought to be the best part of a man's life is not a platitude. It is a conviction based on personal observation and personal experience. Allow me to repeat: by the time we enter middle age most of us have already achieved social and financial security or are well on the way to doing so, and we are starting to enjoy the freedom that comes when children grow up and begin fending for themselves.

> We are free of the need to prove ourselves, which makes the twenties and thirties such a stressful time of life. We are free of the need to push and shove as we climb our career ladder. We are free, or soon will be, of the financial burden and other obligations of having children at school. We are free to start doing the things which we always wanted to do but for which we somehow never had enough time or money. In short, middle age should be the time when you start receiving the pay-off from the previous hard slog.

In some ways, life as we live it seems back to front. When we are young and have the time and energy to do things, we don't have the money. After that, while we are raising a family and buying a house, we have neither the time nor the money. Then comes middle age. At last we have the time and the money to play golf regularly again, or to join a bushwalking club as we always planned to do, or to go on that often-talked-about trip to Gallipoli, or to finally teach ourselves the guitar, or to start spending weekends away. The tragedy is that many of us are no longer fit enough, active enough, healthy enough or energetic enough to do any of these things.

I have no grandchildren as yet, but I look forward very much to having them and doing things with them. I suspect there are many men of about my age with sons and daughters that are grown-up or almost grown-up, who now regret not spending more time with them while they were children. The reason, in my own case, was that I was away playing cricket for many months each year. Career commitments no doubt affected many other men in the same way. Middle age offers the opportunity to make amends for previous omissions by spending a lot of time with your grandchildren, but, again, to do this you have to be mobile enough to keep up with them, physically and mentally.

CHAPTER NINETEEN
THE FITNESS GOAL

We exercise for the benefit of our bodies, of course, but we should not overlook the feel-good factor.

THE GREAT THING ABOUT FITNESS in middle age is that it is not so hard to achieve. What you have to do is change your eating habits, walk regularly and exercise regularly. You do not have to enrol at a gym or invest in expensive exercising equipment. We have all seen those exercise machines advertised on television. Millions of dollars have been spent on these contraptions and most of them are rusting in the garage. As I will explain later in Chapter 21, for $20 or less you can build a home gym that will provide everything you need.

There are three ways to prolong your active middle age:

- ***Eat nutritious food.***
- ***Keep fit.***
- ***Take supplements.***

This has all been said before, but it is important enough to be worth repeating. The vital subject of nutrition has occupied most of the preceding chapters. Let us look now at how a middle-aged man ought to get fit and keep fit.

In the late 1990s very few middle-aged men are naturally fit.

The need to make a special effort to keep fit is one of the penalties of modern living. There was a time when people got all the exercise they needed in their normal daily lives. The late Hunter 'Stork' Hendry, who played Test cricket for Australia in the 1920s, was once asked if the great fast bowlers of his day, Ted McDonald and Jack Gregory, spent a lot of time training. Hendry's reply was remarkable. He said that apart from bowling in the nets McDonald and Gregory did no training at all. He could not remember either of them running a single lap of the oval, much less working out in whatever kind of gyms were available then.

Hendry then made an important observation. He pointed out that McDonald and Gregory lived far more active lives than young men of modern times. They would have climbed stairs instead of using lifts and escalators, cut lawns with push mowers, walked to the local shop instead of driving, walked to the post box instead of sending a fax, and quite possibly walked to and from work. They did not need to run around the oval. They were naturally fit.

In the late 1990s very few middle-aged men are naturally fit. Fitness is a condition we can attain only by exercising. You could fill a library with the books and articles that have been written over the past twenty years on this subject. The number of exercise programs they contain must run into thousands. I intend to suggest just one. The program is designed for middle-age men, and the reason I suggest it is that it has worked for me.

There are three parts to the program.

- ***One consists of walking, which I do three or four times a week.***
- ***The second consists of muscle toning, which I try to do every day.***
- ***The third consists of exercise routines, mainly stretches, which I do first thing in the morning and last thing at night.***

In the next few chapters we will look at each of these in turn.

We exercise for the benefit of our bodies, of course, but we should not overlook the feel-good factor. Most men who exercise regularly, myself included, experience it to some degree—an ongoing feeling of personal satisfaction and wellbeing. It is not an easy feeling to define, but when it is present it is unmistakable. You feel good about yourself, you feel more alive, you feel invigorated. Nobody knows for sure if it has a chemical or psychological origin, but this does not really matter. The important thing is that exercising not only does you good but also makes you feel good.

There is a converse to all this. When you don't exercise, you feel bad about yourself. You keep thinking to yourself: 'You lazy bastard, why don't you get up and go for a walk?' So you live with a vague feeling of guilt, which over a period must have a negative effect on your attitude to yourself and to your outlook on life in general.

Exercise can have a strangely invigorating effect in the short term, too. Here is something I have discovered: if you come home feeling worn out and throw yourself into a chair, you will continue to feel worn out. But if, instead, you jump up and do ten minutes' vigorous walking or exercising—admittedly the last thing you would ordinarily feel like doing in this situation—the feeling of exhaustion disappears.

I know the idea of exercising to overcome exhaustion sounds contradictory, but I have tried it many times and have not known it to fail. There is one precondition, of course: you must be reasonably fit to start with.

Your heart and your age: an alarming link

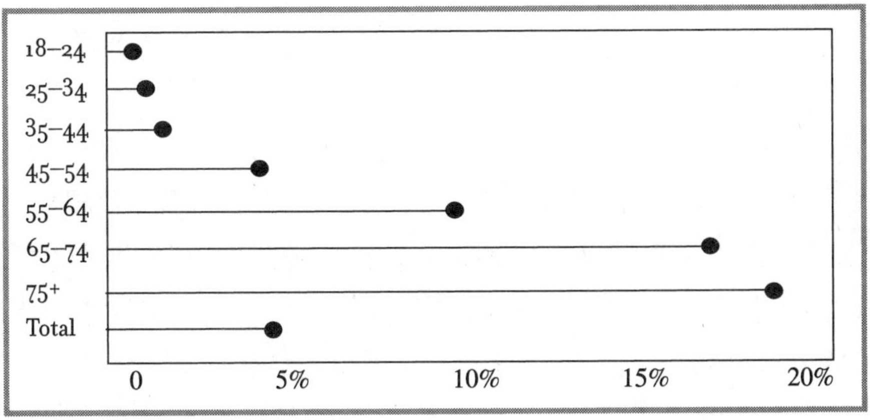

Regular aerobic exercise such as walking is one of our best protections against heart disease, which makes it of immense importance to middle-aged men—as this chart illustrates. The chart shows how the percentage of men with heart disease rises sharply in middle age. (Source: Australian Bureau of Statistics)

Exercise produces valuable health benefits other than aerobic fitness. For instance, every exercise you do increases the blood flow and also the level of oxygen in the blood, which is good for the body as a whole. Lately there has been rising interest in the importance of oxygen levels. A lot of research has been done on the subject, and recently new health products have been launched in the United States which are intended to raise the levels. It is a subject we are likely to hear more of in the next few years.

THE WHEREWITHAL TO BE ACTIVE

Since turning forty, I have changed from being someone who exercised in fits and starts as my enthusiasm for it waxed and waned to someone who sticks to a program faithfully, month after month. Frankly, I would not dare do otherwise. I recognise that as a middle-aged man I have reached a stage in life where I need to keep active if I want to remain active. If I were to get lazy and go for a month or two without exercising, I know I would be on a downhill slide. The slide might start slowly, but with each month it would get steeper and steeper and before long I would be joining the ranks of clapped-out middle-aged men. True, I could always stop the slide and start exercising again, but I would have lost valuable ground and to recover that lost ground would not be easy.

The walking routine and the exercises described in the next few chapters are therefore not intended as a quick fix for the unfit. They are a program for the long haul. You really need to follow them or some similar program for the rest of your life. If you do, the quality of your life will be immeasurably better and you will be happy living longer. There is little to be said for living twenty years longer if for most of this time you are unwell and find it hard to get around. All you will have managed to do is extend your old age. But if you extend your life by twenty years by extending your middle age by twenty years, then it will be a longer life worth living.

CHAPTER TWENTY
WALKING: THE PREFERABLE ALTERNATIVE

By walking, you enjoy most of the health benefits of running without incurring the health risks of running.

MIKE AGOSTINI, the former sprint champion and fitness expert, wrote a book called *How To Avoid Killing Yourself: The Dangers of Being a Fitness Fanatic.* It contains a special warning for people who are inactive in their twenties and thirties and then, on reaching middle age (which Agostini loosely defines as passing the age of forty), suddenly decide to try to get fit again. He warns some will have developed coronary disease between the ages of twenty and forty and not be aware of it, so they risk killing themselves in the attempt. They also risk injuring or even maiming themselves. Agostini cites research showing that middle-aged people should not exercise hard on any two consecutive days, the reason being that the middle-aged body takes up to thirty-six hours to fully recover from this kind of exercise.

This is consistent with my own experience. When I cast my mind back over people I knew of roughly my own age who have died over the past ten years or so, I am surprised at how many of them died running. In fact, most of those who died suddenly in this age bracket died running. The statistics support this impression. Some time ago an American survey was reported in the press which showed that a surprisingly high proportion of men who died suddenly between the ages of forty and sixty died while running or having sex. I mentioned this to a middle-aged friend, a former cricketer. 'I'd better give up running,' he said.

Some studies have suggested that a man of fifty-eight can indeed be fitter and thus, in effect, 'younger' than one aged twenty-eight.

Mile Agostini's overall message is nevertheless positive. He writes: 'Some studies have suggested that a man of fifty-eight can indeed be fitter and thus, in effect, 'younger' than one aged twenty-eight if the older person maintains a sound fitness regime while the other does little or nothing.' I agree entirely. I am fitter now in an overall sense than I was when I played cricket for Australia. Many other active, middle-aged men could say the same thing.

I would not try too hard to persuade a middle-aged man who has been running for years to stop it. But I would certainly try to persuade a middle-aged man who has been inactive for years not to take it up. This isn't just because of the obvious risk of having a heart attack or damaging joints. There are other, little-recognised health risks inherent in vigorous exertion in middle age. One is potential damage from chemical particles in the body called free radicals, which are discussed at length in Chapter 26. Free radicals can cause disease and otherwise harm the body in countless ways, and strenuous exercise is known to accelerate their intake and their production by the body. This is a particularly important consideration in middle age, when the body's natural defence against free radicals has begun to weaken.

A much preferable alternative is brisk walking. By walking, you enjoy most of the health benefits of running without incurring the health risks of running. There is evidence to show that even in middle age you need to walk for at least twenty minutes to make the exercise really worthwhile, although my own view is that a ten-minute or even five-minute walk is much better than nothing.

Dr Ken Cooper, the American doctor and author who helped launch the fitness craze in the late 1960s, argues in his latest book, *The Antioxidant Revolution*, that fast walking is the most effective form of exercise, one of the reasons being the danger of free-radical damage from high-intensity exercise. He also points out that a really fast walker—that is, one who can go as fast as a jogger—actually burns off more calories per kilometre than the jogger.

I do no running at all, but I do a lot of walking. I normally play golf twice a week, which ensures I get a good walk on at least two days in seven, and on top of this I try to walk for twenty minutes or more on at least two other days.

Ideally, you ought to walk briskly to lift your pulse rate and exercise your heart. For the same reason, try to include a hill or two in your route—

provided, of course, you are up to it. You should not puff yourself out, though. You need not exert yourself to a point where you cannot talk while you walk.

...a really fast walker—that is, one who can go as fast as a jogger—actually burns off more calories per kilometre than the jogger.

As we all know, walking burns up energy and so burns up fat—provided you do it regularly. A brisk walk raises our metabolic rate by more than most of us realise. Oxygen intake is probably the best measure of this. If you are sitting in a chair, your body will probably be using about a third of a litre of oxygen per minute. If you get out of the chair and stride down the street, the rate of usage is likely to climb to one and a third litres of oxygen per minute; that is, three to four times as much. For many years scientists have believed that the body's metabolic rate remained higher than normal long after the exercise was finished, a phenomenon which was sometimes referred to as 'after glow'. Thus, a twenty-minute walk a day ensured that your body burned up fat for, say, twenty-four hours. Unfortunately, research at Flinders University in South Australia by the sports scientist Dr Christopher Gore has all but debunked this theory. Dr Gore found that the 'after glow' effect of walking or even running was minimal.

This may be disappointing for walkers, yet, as Dr Gore himself says, it does not alter the fact that, apart from other benefits such as the reduced risk of cardiovascular disease, regular walking combined with a healthy food intake helps you control body weight. The key word here is 'regular'. Dr Gore's research shows that it takes thirty half-hour walks to burn off one kilogram of body fat. In other words, if you were to walk for thirty minutes a day on five days a week it would take you six weeks to burn off a kilogram of fat. This may seem slow progress, but it also means that if you did it for a year you would burn off nearly nine kilograms, or about a stone and a half. Of course, if you also take action on the nutrition front by reducing your intake of fat and protein, your weight may drop much faster.

WHEN AND WHERE

Walking is an idiosyncratic activity. Some men like to follow exactly the same route around surrounding streets and parks, year in year out. Others like to vary the route each time they set off. Some prefer to walk early in the morning before showering and dressing for work. Others prefer the cool of the evening and, perhaps, the cover of darkness.

My general reservation about exercise machines is that when the novelty wears off, the machine disappears into the garage.

A journalist friend of mine who tried and failed for years to settle into a regular walking routine finally had success when he bought a Walkman-style radio and began listening to tapes of classical music as he walked around.

From then on, he says, his daily walk became not a task but a pleasure.

Then there are those who exercise in probably the most efficient way of all—they walk to and from work. Presumably they are people with access to showering and changing facilities at the office. I once read of a Sydney man who walked from his home in Mosman to his office in St Leonards every morning and then walked home at night. Anyone with a knowledge of this part of Sydney will appreciate just how long a walk this is, yet the person concerned insisted he got there quicker than he could have by peak-hour bus.

Some middle-aged men prefer using machines such as exercise bikes and treadmills to walking. This is fine, provided they keep at it. My general reservation about exercise machines (apart from the fact that they can cost a lot of money) is that the people who use them often do not persist with them. When the novelty wears off, the machine disappears into the garage, never to be seen again.

THE REBOUNDER

There is one machine I do recommend. It is a small, circular trampoline known variously as a rebounder, rebound jogger or simply mini-trampoline. You need to buy one that is reasonably strong (the springs tend to give out in the cheaper models), but even so you will probably not have to pay more than $80. Jogging on a rebounder is an excellent alternative to walking when walking is difficult, perhaps because the weather is too hot, too cold or too wet. It is a good idea to buy one and put

Jogging on the rebounder is an excellent exercise and it does not jar the knees and ankles.

it on the floor next to the chair where you normally sit to watch television. If there is a half-hour show that you watch each night—the news, for instance—make a point of dragging your rump out of the chair and jogging on the rebounder while you watch the television. You need not do anything strenuous. If it suits you, just imitate the shuffle that Cliff Young used on his long-distance runs.

Jogging on the rebounder is an excellent exercise and it does not jar the knees and ankles. There can be no excuse for not doing it, either, for everyone can spare at least a half-hour per day to watch television. There may well be an extra health benefit, too. Each time your body rises off the rebounder there is said to be a momentary period of weightlessness, which aids the flow in your lymphatic system.

I began using a rebounder while I was in my thirties—years before I began walking regularly. When I turned forty, I went to a clinic to get an executive fitness test done. After the test I sat opposite the specialist in charge of the clinic while he filled out a form with my results. The last part of the form to be filled in was headed 'Body Age', and naturally I was very interested to see what he would write. In fact, he wrote 'forty'. I was disappointed. As a former international sportsman who had been playing golf regularly and using the rebounder, I was immodest enough to believe that my body was young for its years. I thought he might have written 'thirty-two' or, at worst, 'thirty-five'.

He noticed my disappointment and asked what was the matter. I told him I had hoped for a better result. 'I wouldn't worry if I were you,' he said. 'I test a lot of forty-year-olds here, and for most of them I have to write fifty-four or sixty-two. You're miles ahead of the game. You must do a lot of running, do you?' I told him that, no, I didn't run, but I did use a rebounder. 'Well, whatever you're doing,' he said, 'keep doing it, because it works.'

I did keep doing it. I am still using a rebounder today.

CHAPTER TWENTY-ONE

MUSCLE BUILDING

The primary objective is not to develop bigger muscles today but to preserve the muscles you already have for the future.

A MAN IN HIS TWENTIES or thirties can live like a slob and still look reasonably good, because his muscles and skeletal structure are young enough to maintain a respectable body shape. Beyond the age of forty, though, the way you live begins to show up in the way you look. If you fail to exercise your muscles they will start to visibly waste away. This is why even active middle-aged men can look scrawny or flabby from the waist up. They do enough walking to keep their legs well-muscled, but their upper body gets almost no exercise. This results in the familiar droop you see in middle-aged men: the chest sinks, the shoulders narrow and sag, the arms lose their muscular contours.

To prevent this happening, you must either take up some regular activity that gives the upper body a vigorous workout or you must do weights or some equivalent exercise. As we all know, doing weights does involve a risk of injury—especially for someone over the age of forty. By all means do weights in a gym under supervision, but if you do them at home make sure that what you are doing is safe.

My own preference is not to do weights, as such, at all. Instead, I do chin-ups and pull-ups on a bar at my home. There could hardly be a simpler exercise than this, yet it is extremely effective in toning virtually every muscle in my upper body. I got the idea from Nigel Websdale, a fitness expert who has worked with sports people such as Pat Cash, whom I got to know some years ago. I asked him to suggest a set of simple exercises that I could do regularly to keep my upper body in shape. I made it clear to him that I had no ambition to achieve athlete-type fitness. I simply wanted to keep myself in reasonable health and in reasonable shape for the rest of my life.

Even so, I expected to be told to go out and buy a bench and weights or some other state-of-the-art body-building gear. Nigel said forget it. The only equipment I needed to obtain was a piece of galvanised iron pipe. I then had to find some place in or around my home where I could fasten it securely enough to bear my weight. The bar should be positioned well above head height, preferably about level with the fingertips when the arms are held aloft.

Chin-ups and pull-ups: The chin-ups I do are of the traditional type. I do them with an underhand grip on the bar; that is, with the palms of my hands facing me. The pull-ups are virtually the same exercise, except that I have the palms facing away. Between them, these two exercises ensure that all the muscles in the arms, chest and shoulders get a workout. Make sure you breathe out when you pull yourself up, then breathe in as you lower yourself.

Knee-raises: Here is a third exercise I do on the bar every second morning which is a variation of the others. Hang from the bar with outstretched arms and repeatedly raise your knees to waist height. This simple exercise tones up the abdominal muscles as well as the lower back, thighs and buttocks. Raise your knees in three directions in turn:

- one, straight up so they are pointing directly ahead;
- two, at an angle to the left (towards mid-wicket, as a cricketer would say);
- three, at an angle to the right (towards extra cover).

The reason for doing this is that it means all muscles, right across the abdomen, get exercised.

This exercise is particularly valuable if you are trying to get rid of a pot belly. As such, it offers an alternative to sit-ups and other abdominal exercises.

Do not pull your knees up rapidly. You will derive maximum benefit from this exercise if you raise and lower them slowly. Also, as with the chin-ups and pull-ups, breathe out when you do the hard bit (raising your knees) and breathe in when you lower them. The reason you do this is to prevent pressure building up inside the body. If you breathe in or just hold your breath when you exert yourself, your blood pressure will rise and you will also build up pressure in the lungs and abdomen. Breathing out releases the pressure.

I do one of these three exercises each day in a three-day cycle, which means I spend no more than five minutes on them per day, including the short breaks between the various sets. I do chin-ups one day, pull-ups next day, knee-raises the day after that. There is a good reason for doing them in rotation like this. Physiologists tell us that the process of toning our muscles occurs in two stages. In the first stage, the muscle is broken down by overwork during the exercise itself. In the second, the muscle recovers and grows after the exercise. In other words, the improvement is actually achieved after the exercise is over. So if you exercise the same set of muscles every day, you will not derive as much benefit as you will from a three- or four-day rotation. The muscles of even top endurance athletes go through a recovery phase after competing. For people taking part in an iron man event, for instance, the recovery phase can be as long as two weeks.

If you have not done any heavy lifting for some time, you may well struggle to do more than one or two chin-ups or pull-ups to start with. No matter how few you can manage at first, make sure you do not do them all at once but, rather, break them up into several sets. For instance, let us imagine eight chin-ups are about the most you can manage in one go. Then begin by doing a set of five. After this, rest for a couple of minutes before doing another set—let's say of four chin-ups. Rest again, and then do a third and final set of three or maybe only two.

Gradually, you will increase both the number per set and the number of sets. Having done the exercise for years, I can comfortably manage a total of ten chin-ups or pull-ups, spread over four to five sets. I could do more than this with a greater effort, but I feel this is quite sufficient for the purpose. Your own comfortable limit is unlikely to be exactly the same as mine, but whether it is bigger or smaller does not really matter, provided the muscles get the exercise.

I do the knee-raises in the same way. I do a total of sixty to seventy spread over three to four sets, which is as many as anyone of my age needs to do. Remember to vary the direction in which you raise your knees. If you have not done the exercise before, you may well find that ten or twelve will pull you up at first. Keep at it, and you ought to be able to increase the number bit by bit.

Chin-ups: better than weights

Chin-ups and pull-ups have one important advantage over weights: they are less likely to result in injuries to muscles and ligaments, for the simple reason you never have to lift more than your body weight. If the strain becomes too great, you simply won't be able to pull yourself up. In other words, if you can't do it you won't do it. Another big advantage is the simplicity of it all. With a piece of iron pipe a metre long you can create your own home gym. In Canberra my exercise bar was suspended from a pergola at the back of the house. If you are even half a handyman you should have no trouble installing one somewhere inside or outside your home, and the total cost of the materials you need—the length of pipe plus maybe a few screws and brackets—will probably be less than $20.

I am never particularly conscious of the benefits of these exercises while I am doing them, but when I don't do them for a week or more because I am away on a trip, I soon notice the difference. I can feel the loss of strength, muscle tone and bulk in and around my shoulders. Whenever I lose weight I tend to lose it first around the shoulders, so the exercises on the bar are all the more important for me.

Not long ago I spent the best part of a month travelling. I worked for twelve days in Bangladesh on a cricket broadcast, came home for a day, went to Fiji for three days, came home for two days, then spent five days in New Zealand. During the whole of that period I did no exercises at all on the bar. By the end of it I felt almost frail. It seemed to me that a strong wind would have blown me away. Yet after just one week back on the exercise bar I felt like Arnold Schwarzenegger. I did not look like him, but I felt like him.

> Feeling good as a result of exercising is actually very important. It is the carrot your body dangles in front of you: it gives you the incentive to keep going. So you exercise more because it makes you feel good, and all the while your body is reaping the benefit.

I personally believe that chin-ups and pull-ups are ideal for the particular needs of middle-aged men, especially the majority of us who shy away from the idea of going to a gym. Most of us past the age of forty, quite sensibly, have given up the idea of trying to build up our bodies for the sake of appearance, and while these exercises on the bar may be muscle-building they are certainly not meant to be a form of body-building. The primary objective is not to develop bigger muscles today but to preserve the muscles you already have for the future.

You will be amazed at how quickly you notice a difference. You will feel the muscles in your shoulders and arms developing and you will feel stronger because of it. You will see the extra muscle in the mirror, too, which may appeal to your vanity to some degree.

I do the muscle-toning exercises with the same long-term objective in mind that I have referred to many times in this book. Twenty or thirty years from now I aim to have enough strength in my upper body to do all the things I still want to do, one of which, I am sure, will be to make the golf ball fly off the tee instead of just bunting it along the fairway.

CHAPTER TWENTY-TWO
Exercises

Exercises do make a difference. They produce a real, practical benefit which can significantly affect your wellbeing.

For some reason, most people have an aversion to doing exercises. They may be willing to change their eating habits and walk four times a week, but suggest to them that they spend five minutes a day doing exercises and at once they lose interest. The reason, probably, is that most people do not really believe that exercises do them any good. They view them as a kind of ritual which people do out of a sense of duty but which actually produce little, if any, practical benefit. They are wrong. Exercises do make a difference. They produce a real, practical benefit which can significantly affect your wellbeing. I say this as someone who did no regular exercises until five years ago. Doing exercises has certainly made a big difference to me. I know it, because I have felt it.

For those who do not have an exercise program of their own to follow, this chapter details of the exercises I do myself. They were given to me by Joseph Oros, the man who, as I will explain in Chapter 24, introduced Judy and me to vegetarianism. They are not fitness exercises in the

Stretching elongates the muscle fibres, which is one reason it is so effective in maintaining flexibility.

popular meaning of the word, although they certainly aid my fitness. Many of them are essentially stretching exercises—yoga exercises, in fact. What they are intended to do is keep all my moving parts in good working order. They are invaluable in preserving the body's flexibility, which is one of the first things that middle-aged men start to lose. They are meant to ease the various parts of the body (especially the backbone) back into position and, by strengthening the surrounding muscles, to keep them there and so keep the body in shape.

If you own a cat, you will already know a good deal about stretching. Cats stretch themselves many times each day, and like everything else animals do by instinct there is a good reason for it. Stretching elongates the muscle fibres, which is one reason it is so effective in maintaining flexibility. Stretching also tends to calm the mind. Stretching relaxes muscles and so has an overall relaxing effect on the body. This in turn produces a general feeling of wellbeing. Five minutes of stretching in the middle of a busy day can do wonders for your disposition.

Every day I try to do some stretching, preferably at a time when I need to get away from it all, even for a few minutes. When I was running a company in Sydney a few years ago I used to spend five minutes stretching during office hours each day. I soon worked out that the only way to make sure I did it every day was to allocate the time for it in my diary. In other words, I made an appointment for myself to do it. At the chosen moment, usually early in the afternoon, I would close the door, lie on the floor and go through a series of stretching exercises.

I also used to lie there, breathing deeply and allowing myself to relax and drift off into that twilight zone between being awake and asleep. I found this brief period of total relaxation had an energising effect on me. At the end of it I would feel charged up and ready to go again.

The exercises are in two groups. Those in the first group are meant to be done in the morning before you get out of bed and afterwards in the shower. The second can be done in your office or at home at the end of the day. (Personally, I try to do them in both situations: in the office in the afternoon and again at home in the evening.)

There is a reason, apart from convenience, for doing exercises in bed in the morning. Basically, the exercises are intended to reset your spine and joints while your body is at its most relaxed. The hip exercises loosen up the lower back, a vulnerable area for most middle-aged men, especially if they spend most of their working day sitting. The evening exercises tend to relax the body, so if you do them just before turning in they will help you get a good night's rest.

The important thing is that all the following exercises must be done slowly and thoroughly. Try to keep this in mind at all times.

Morning program

There are eight sets of exercises which can be done in bed. I suggest that for the first couple of weeks while you are getting used to the exercises and while your pelvic area is still in the process of being loosened up that you confine yourself to the first set. In the third week do both the first and second sets. Thereafter, you could do all the exercises, one after the other, in the order they appear here.

Exercise One

Aim: to loosen the hips, lower back and spine

1. Remove your pillow and lie flat on your back on the bed, with your legs straight and your hands palms-down and close to your side. Your fingers should be together and your toes pointing up.
2. Starting from the hip, slide your left leg slowly down past your right leg then slide it back. It is important to get this movement right, because it is the basis of many of the exercises that follow. What you are doing is pushing the leg downwards from the hip so that it extends for a few centimetres beyond the other leg. The movement at the hip is the key to it. If you lie down on the floor and try it, you will understand at once what is involved. As you slide the leg down, you will feel your lower backbone engaged. What is happening here is that the muscles around the backbone are being stretched and the backbone flexed. If your backbone happens to be slightly displaced (actually a common occurrence) you can gently jiggle it back by

repeating this exercise. This is what is meant by 'resetting the backbone'.

3. Repeat with the right leg. Slowly do the exercise fourteen times with each leg.

Exercise Two

Aim: to reset the spine and stretch the body gently

1. As well as sliding your left leg slowly down past the other, roll it inwards from the hip as if you were trying to touch the mattress with the inside of your foot. This is hard to do at first and you may take a few weeks to master it. Don't force the foot down. Just roll from the hip.
2. Repeat with right leg. Do the exercise slowly seven times with each leg.

Exercise Three

Aim: to stretch the lower back

1. Lie flat on the bed and place both middle fingers on the pubic bone. (The fingers are put there purely as markers so you can see the pubic bone moving. They are not meant to play any part in the movement.) Thrust the pubic bone upwards—that is, as if you were trying to lift it towards your navel—without lifting your buttocks off the bed. Hold it there for a few seconds and release. Repeat three times.
2. With your middle fingers still in place, move the pubic bone in the

other direction; that is, tilt it downwards and forwards. Hold it there for a few seconds and release. Remember, the hips are not meant to be raised in this exercise.

Exercise Four

Aim: to stretch the lower legs

1. Bend both knees and place your feet flat on the bed, with your hands palm-down by your side and the fingers together.
2. Squeeze toes down into mattress, then relax. Repeat three times.
3. Flex the toes upward, then relax. Repeat three times.

Exercise Five

Aim: to reset major organs

1. Bend both knees and place your hands on the front of your abdomen with the fingers pointing down towards the pubic area.
2. Breathe in slowly through your nose, allowing your torso to expand. Breathe out slowly, allowing the torso to collapse. Repeat three times.

Exercise Six

Aim: to exercise the eyes

1. Lie flat on the bed with the legs straight and flat and your eyes closed. Blink both eyes five times and then squeeze them firmly, keeping them squeezed for a few seconds. Release and repeat five times.

2. With the eyes still closed, look in turn upwards, to the right, downwards and to the left. Repeat five times in one direction (say, clockwise) and five times in the other (anticlockwise).
3. Repeat steps 1 and 2 with eyes open.

Exercise Seven

Aim: To exercise the neck

1. Lying flat on the bed with your hands by your side and your toes pointing up, rotate your neck slowly to the right as far as comfortable before returning slowly to the starting point.
2. Rotate neck slowly to left as far as comfortable, then return to the starting point.
3. Repeat fourteen times each side.

Exercise Eight

Aim: To stretch the neck and reset the top half of the spine

1. Lie flat on the bed with your shoulders in line with the end of the bed and your head hanging down over the end of the bed. This loosens the top half of the backbone.
2. Raise your head slowly to the level of the bed, then lower it slowly. Repeat five times. On alternate days roll your head slowly from side to side while your head is hanging back. Repeat five times.
3. With your head hanging over the end of the bed, push your toes slowly towards the mattress and hold for a few seconds. Repeat three times.

4. Pull your toes slowly in the other direction (that is, towards your head) and hold them there for a few seconds. Repeat three times.

5. Having hung your head over the end of the bed, raise it to the level of the bed while, at the same time, sliding your left leg past the right and rolling it inwards as in Exercise Two. Then, as you lower your head, return your left leg to its starting position and slide the right leg past the left, rolling it inwards from the hip. (Although this may sound complicated, you are simply doing the leg slides, as in Exercises One and Two, and raising and lowering your head at the same time.)

6. Place your hands on either side of your abdomen with the fingers pointing down, breathe in slowly through the nostrils, allowing the torso to expand, and hold for a few seconds. Then release slowly, allowing the torso to collapse. Repeat three times.

7. With your head still over the end of the bed, raise your legs, bending the knees first, until they are at right angles to the bed; that is, fairly straight and pointing upwards. Slide your left leg from the hip past the right leg, return it, and then slide the right leg slowly from hip past the left. Repeat seven times each side. Again, you are simply doing the leg slides of Exercises One and Two except that here you are doing them with your legs in the air. This exercise also helps strengthen the abdomen and lower back.

8. With your head still over the end of the bed, bend your knees and place your feet flat on the bed with your hands by your side and the fingers together. Squeeze your toes downwards three times, then pull upwards three times.

9. Repeat steps 6 and 7.

10. Move your body down until your head is back on the bed and raise your legs until they are at right angles to the bed. Then slide each leg from the hip seven times in turn. One objective here is to allow you to recover from the effects of hanging your head over the bed and so prevent dizziness if you stand up after the exercises.

Shower Exercise

Aim: to loosen the hip, pelvic and lower-back areas, to strengthen the abdominal area and to stretch the hamstrings

1. Standing under a hot shower (the heat helps the muscle stretching), bend forwards from your waist with your legs straight, your arms crossed and your hands on opposite shoulders. Position yourself so that the water is running over your lower back.

2. Keeping each leg straight—that is, the movement has to be initiated at the hip—lift each heel off the floor in turn and repeat seven times.

3. While still bent over, breathe in slowly and try to move your abdomen around in a circular motion. (At least have the mental image of doing it.) Do it clockwise for a full circle and hold. Reverse the procedure in an anticlockwise direction. Repeat three times. This helps to reposition the organs in this area.

4. Then allow your shoulders and torso to relax and drop forward, stretching your lower back and hamstrings for a slow count of seven.

LATE AFTERNOON/EVENING PROGRAM

Exercise One

Aim: to stretch the backbone, which after a day's sitting is probably locked, and to loosen the hips

1. Lie flat on the floor with your toes pointing up, your arms and fingers outstretched above your head, as if you were trying to achieve your full height.
2. Sliding your left leg from the hip, slowly rotate it inwards and down past the right leg. Return.
3. Sliding your right leg from the hip, slowly rotate it inwards and down past the left leg. Return.
4. Repeat seven times with each leg.

Exercise Two

Aim: to stretch the body, exercise the arm muscles and, by clenching and unclenching the fist, to pump blood through the arms

1. Lie flat on the floor with your toes pointing up and your hands clenched by your sides.
2. While slowly sliding each leg in turn from the hips, raise your arms over your head to full height, clenching and unclenching your fists as the arms swing over as if you were squeezing a squash ball. Return

your arms to your sides slowly, clenching and unclenching fists and sliding legs alternately. The fist may be clenched and unclenched ten times each time the arm swings over. Breathe in each time you slide a different leg, allowing the torso to expand. Raise your arms overhead and return three times.

Exercise Three

Aim: to strengthen the abdomen and lower back

1. While still lying flat on floor, lift each leg in turn until it is at right angles to the floor, keeping the leg as straight as possible, and hold it there for a few seconds. Repeat three times with each leg.
2. Lift both legs together to right angles with the bed, keeping the knees as straight as possible. Hold for a few seconds, then slowly lower. Repeat three times.
3. Lift both legs together to right angles with the bed, hold briefly, then slide each leg in turn slowly from the hip. Repeat seven times with each leg.

Exercise Four

Aim: to strengthen the buttocks, lower back and abdominal area

1. Roll over onto your stomach and place your hands by your side.
2. Raise your left leg—that is, heel first—as far as comfortable and hold it there for a few seconds. Return to the starting position.

3. Raise your right leg as far as comfortable and hold it there for a few seconds. Return.

4. With your hands by your side, raise both legs together, heels first, and hold for a few seconds. Return. Repeat three times.

5. With your hands behind your back and head and both legs raised, rock backwards and forwards as often as possible, working up towards a target of fifty. Return to the starting position. This exercise produces a reverse flexing of the backbone and so strengthens the muscles.

6. Stretch your arms over your head, cross the arms at the wrist and cross the legs at the ankles, then stretch your body for a slow count of five. Relax.

Exercise Five

Aim: to stretch and strengthen the stomach and lower back muscles

1. Roll over onto your back. Cross your arms, place your hands on opposite shoulders and straighten your legs.

2. Try to sit up by raising your body from the shoulders; that is, try to do a sit-up. If you can manage it, repeat it seven times. If it proves too difficult, however, bend your knees and raise the shoulders as far as comfortable and hold them there for a few seconds before relaxing. Repeat seven times. You should be able to do the sit-ups as you gets stronger.

3. Sit with your legs extended straight ahead. Lean forward and grip your toes. Pull the body slowly forward by pulling your toes down towards the floor, then back towards you. Repeat twenty-eight times. If this proves too difficult, extend the arms forward with outstretched fingers and slowly work your torso towards your toes. Repeat twenty-eight times.

4. Lie on your back, lift your legs above you, keeping them straight, and reach up to grip your toes. Then, by rocking backwards and forwards, try to touch your toes on the floor behind your head. Don't force this to begin with. In time your neck will become more flexible.

5. Kneel on the floor and sit upright on your heels with your hands in your lap and your arms relaxed. Allow your head to fall forwards so that your chin rests on your chest. Slowly roll your head in a circular motion. Do it three times clockwise and three times anticlockwise.

6. Still kneeling, sit upright on your heels with your hands together in prayer position above your head. Keeping your elbows out, try to touch shoulder blades together for a slow count of twenty-eight.

7. Still kneeling, place your hands behind you and lower your body backwards as far as comfortable. You should aim eventually to be able to sit on the floor; that is, to place your buttocks on the floor between your feet. In time, when doing this last exercise, you should be able to lie back with your body right on the floor. If you have any kind of back problem, though, you should obtain professional advice beforehand about the suitability of this exercise.

Exercise Six

Aim: to loosen the lower torso, buttocks and lower back

1. Lie flat on your back, bend your knees and place your arms above your head with the elbows up, the palms of your hands on the mattress and your fingers spread. Your hands should now be about level with your head. Using your legs, hands and head as supports, raise your torso off the floor and create a kind of table top with your body. Relax and repeat three times.

Exercise Seven

Aim: to reset all parts of the body by reversing the pull of gravity, to strengthen the neck muscles, to produce a big flow of blood to the brain and to revitalise sluggish organs by reversing the blood flow

1. Position yourself near a wall or some other solid support and do a handstand; that is, stand upside down on your hands with your legs pointed upwards and supported by the wall. Hold the position for as long as comfortable. Ideally, start the handstand by facing the wall and then flipping your legs above you. If this too difficult, face away from the wall, get down on your hands and knees and work your legs up the wall behind you.
2. After a few weeks of doing handstands you should be able to do a headstand. You can cushion your head either on a firm, flat cushion (not a soft one) or on the palms of your hands laid on the floor, palms

up and fingers intertwined. Then flip or work your legs up the wall as previously described. Hold the position for as long as comfortable. Aim to increase the duration of the head stand to a few minutes. To avoid dizziness after you have finished, always rest with your head below the level of your heart for a few minutes before standing up. This exercise, like the previous one, allows organs which have sagged towards the bottom of your torso to return to their normal positions. It also revitalises them by reversing the blood flow.

CHAPTER TWENTY-THREE
MAKING TIME

Your fitness and your health are far, far too important to be treated as an expendable filler which you squeeze in somewhere when you have spare time.

BY AND LARGE, WE ARE all too busy being busy. We live our lives at what seems to us a hectic pace, which we then use as an excuse for failing to do a lot of things we ought to do. If we were to sit down and put on paper everything we have left undone recently, most of us could fill a page. Our list would include all sorts of everyday items, each of them important in its own way yet none so urgent that it had to be done there and then, so it wasn't done. Making an effort each day to keep fit may not be on everyone's list of omissions, but it ought to be, for the majority of Australian men neglect to do it. Somehow, fitness always seems something we can worry about tomorrow.

The truth is, if we examine our daily schedules honestly, there is plenty of time each day to do all the things we have been putting off. The trouble is we fail to organise our time. The secret of finding time to do something is to make time to do it, not just vaguely hope that time might become available. You have to deliberately set aside time for it. Admittedly there is a limit to how far we can go in putting all our waking hours into various boxes, but our physical fitness—and, therefore, our health—is so important, so vital to our overall wellbeing, that we have to make a box for it. It must be written into the daily schedule.

...the man who works so hard that he has no time to devote to his health is grossly irresponsible.

After retiring from cricket I concentrated on my second-favourite game, golf. I played every Saturday, yet, for me, this was not enough. It wasn't enough for me to improve my play, and it wasn't enough to satisfy my appetite for the game. I used to think how wonderful it would be to take Wednesday afternoons off, as many of my golfing friends did, and play in the usual mid-week competition. But I was busy making a career in business at the time and, so I thought, could not possibly afford the time.

One day I happened to mention to a fellow club member how I envied him being able to play on Wednesday. He replied, 'Mate, if you don't plan it, if you don't organise it, you'll never play on Wednesday, because you'll never have enough time.' What he said set me thinking. I went back to the office and had my assistant draw a line through every Wednesday afternoon in my diary for weeks ahead. From then on I played in the Wednesday afternoon comp. It was not really a case of taking time off work to do it. I was already working a sixty-hour week and continued to do so. Rather, it was a case of making time for it.

What I found interesting was the effect this had on the office. For a week or two, it did cause some disruption—a few appointments had to be changed and so on. After that everyone became accustomed to my being absent after midday every Wednesday and my absence made no difference to how the office operated. After all, if you leave the office to attend a meeting or some other appointment that lasts all afternoon, the office will continue to function. There is nothing so important that it cannot wait until the next day or cannot be dealt with by the staff who are there. In other words, my Wednesday afternoon's golf was treated as just another appointment.

What I also found interesting was the effect the afternoon's golf had on me. I am sure I achieved a lot more in a business sense by having that break in the middle of the week, because I always felt rejuvenated after it. While I was on the golf course I was so engrossed in my game that I forgot all my other problems. The Wednesday golf was six hours away from the stress of life, and each week I found myself looking forward to it. I protected that afternoon's golf as if it were a treasured possession, and it took a really exceptional circumstance to make me surrender it.

AN ALTERNATIVE TO THE BUSINESS LUNCH

In another period of my business career I went to a lot of business lunches. I normally left the office at 12.15 p.m. and did not get back until 2.45 p.m. or later. Thus, I was away for at least two and a half hours, yet not once did anything happen during my absence that the office could not handle or could not be dealt with after I got back. At that time I was working in the insurance and fund-management industries, so networking over lunch was sometimes useful. A majority of the lunches, though, were a pure indulgence and, business-wise, produced no benefit. Moreover, they were clearly bad for my health, for most of the meals were full of fat, and over a period they were fairly expensive, too.

So I decided to use the time to better advantage. When I was invited to a business lunch which I considered unnecessary, I declined the invitation but still marked off the two and a half hours in my diary. At 12.15 p.m. on the appointed day, I would head off to the golf course and spend two and a half hours hitting a big bucket of balls on the practice range or, more often, playing nine holes. During those two and a half hours I would get some exercise, practise my golf, obtain some stress relief and spare my digestive system the burden of having to dispose of a big lunch.

The point of all this is that I made time to do it. I made an appointment for myself to enjoy an activity which at that stage of my life was my main form of exercise. This is what you might think of doing, too. If the only time you can walk or exercise is in the morning before you go to work, then get up half an hour earlier to do it. If your reply to this is: 'But I already have to get up at six a.m. to make it to work on time,' then my reply would be, 'So get up at 5.30!' Your fitness and your health are far, far too important to be treated as an expendable filler which you squeeze in somewhere when you have spare time. Make an appointment for yourself, in writing if necessary, to work on your fitness.

There is a crazy logic in the way many men lead their lives. They work flat out all week and so have no time to exercise. Their consciences are clear, because they feel they are doing the right thing by their families: making more money and providing the families with extra material benefits. Their consciences should not be clear, however. By ignoring their health, they are running a significant risk of being stricken by ill health in middle age and, perhaps, dying in their fifties. The dire consequences both for their family and their business, if either possibility were to eventuate, are well known to us all. Viewed in this way, the man who works so hard that he has no time to devote to his health is grossly irresponsible.

CHAPTER TWENTY-FOUR
THE FORTY-DAY DIET

Neither of us had done anything like this before and I was sceptical, to say the least, about my ability to last eight days without solid food.

SOME READERS WILL SKIP this chapter, believing there is no way in the world they could go for eight days without eating anything solid and then another thirty-two days without eating any meat. I can understand that. What follows here is simply not for them.

To those who are interested enough to read on, though, two things ought to be said at the outset.

> **One**, the diet worked wonders for me. In a way, it changed my life. ***Two***, doing it was not nearly as tough as I thought it would be. I am sure it is within the capability of anyone with a moderate amount of willpower—provided they really want to do it.

I should qualify what I just said by pointing out that my wife and I did the diet together. If you are married and your wife is unwilling to cooperate, doing the diet might be a lot more difficult. Fortunately for me, all the dietary changes Judy and I have made since 1979 have been made by us together. We have been both a partner and support for each other. We virtually gave up red meat and dairy products together in 1979, and we largely eliminated these foods from our children's diets, too. I say 'virtually' because we did not give up red meat entirely. I might not have eaten slabs of red meat in the form of, say, a steak or roast lamb, but I still ate meals such as pasta dishes which had red meat in them.

It was Judy who took the first step towards becoming a pure vegetarian. In 1993 she began going regularly to a gym in Canberra to generally tone herself up. This was successful up to a point. She slimmed down a little, but she did not really enjoy the gym work. A few of the regulars at the gym used to meet for a coffee or a juice afterwards, and it was there that Judy met a man named Joseph Oros. He was born and grew up in Hungary and apparently came to Australia as a young man, for he had worked for many years as a plant biologist at the CSIRO.

It emerged later that as a boy Joseph had come under the influence of an Indian, a teacher by profession, who happened to be a vegan and practised yoga. The Indian cooked for the Oros family and was also Joseph's tutor. Under his direction, Joseph became a vegan at the age of eight. Apart from the time he spent in military service, when he had the choice of eating meat-based meals or nothing, he remained a vegan for the rest of his life.

Judy used to chat to Joseph. He was an eccentric character in some ways, and extremely intelligent and likeable. He asked Judy how she found the gym. Judy replied that it seemed to be doing her some good but that she did not particularly enjoy it. She also said she still felt heavy. Joseph began talking to her about the way he ate and the way he exercised. Judy was interested and questioned him further.

Eventually, he suggested she consider going on a forty-day eating program that he would set out for her. It was to be a cleansing diet. For the first eight days she would be on a liquids-only diet and for the other thirty-two on a pure vegetarian diet. It would not be an ordinary vegetarian diet, either. She would have nothing but liquids until the evening, so dinner would be her only solid meal of the day. Joseph promised that at the end of it she would feel better than she had ever felt in her life.

Judy told me about it, and I was interested. She asked me if I would like to meet Joseph. I said I would, and we went to his home. In appearance he was everything you might expect a guru to be, bearded and long-haired. As I later discovered, he was known to walk around Canberra in the middle of winter wearing sandals, cotton trousers and a short-sleeved shirt. There was virtually no furniture in the house. We sat on cushions on the floor with our legs crossed. It was winter, but the only form of heating was a small gas heater (it reminded me of R2D2) in the middle of the lounge room.

My initial impression was negative. Joseph was too unconventional, too way-out, for my personal taste. Fortunately, I made a conscious effort to put this prejudice aside and listen to what he was saying. I soon found myself enthralled. He opened my eyes that day to the true importance of nutrition. Over the previous fourteen years I must have read millions of words, literally, on the subject of food—what we should eat, how much we should eat, when we should eat it. Much of what I had read was fat related. It was about how we could minimise our fat intake and how this would benefit both our appearance and our health. Joseph Oros made me understand that nutrition was of much, much broader importance than this.

In Chapter nine I mentioned that for twenty years or more I had suffered a skin condition, a legacy of all the time I had spent in the sun playing cricket—my three lifetimes in the sun, as I like to refer to it. Essentially, it was a just mild skin infection, but it had resisted attempts by many doctors over the years to cure it. I asked Joseph if he thought his cleansing diet might help my skin problem. He replied that he would be very surprised if the problem did not disappear within a week.

After we left, Judy asked me what I thought of him. I said I was fascinated with what he had to say but was still put off by his eccentricity. Nevertheless, if she wanted to give his diet a go, I was prepared to do it with her. This would make it easier for her and, who knows, it might help my skin condition, too.

The start of the cleansing

So we started. Neither of us had done anything like this before and I was sceptical, to say the least, about my ability to last eight days without solid food. The liquids Joseph prescribed for us were basically a mixture of fruit juices and vegetable broths. These were not selected at random. He was very specific about which juices we should drink and when, and about which vegetables were to be used in the broth. Among them were celeriac (a type of celery) and turnips, which I had rarely, if ever, eaten. The diet was formulated to provide specific vitamins and minerals in specific quantities.

Breakfast consisted of mixed citrus juices (orange, lemon, lime and grapefruit) and lunch of a vegetable broth. We boiled the vegetables, tipped the vegetables out and drank the water. All the nutrients from the vegetables were left in the water, so we were avoiding the bulk of the vegetables but still getting the nutrition.

Dinner in the evening was the same kind of broth, although made from a different combination of vegetables. We also drank certain herbal teas which were meant to nourish the nerve ends. We mixed them with ginseng and honey for energy. The idea was to sip the mixture during the day whenever we felt hungry. To this day, I still make up this herbal tea-ginseng-honey drink every morning and carry it with me in a vacuum flask wherever I go.

Much to my surprise, I got through the eight days quite easily. I attribute this not to any great willpower but to the fact that before I started I got into the right frame of mind to do it. Judy encouraged me to do it, and I fully committed myself to the idea. I felt that if we were doing it at the same time we could give each other moral support, although as things turned out I had to spend five of the eight days away from home on business in Sydney.

Joseph had warned us that after four or five days on the liquid diet we ought to make sure we were never too far from a toilet. He said a moment would come about this time when we would need to reach a toilet not within minutes but within seconds. That moment arrived for me late one day while I was in Sydney. I had left the office but fortunately had already arrived at the place where I was staying. I was no more than twenty paces from the toilet when the message came through like an alarm bell that I needed to go there urgently, and I only just made it. In the next few seconds I felt my body voided itself completely. The experience helped me understand why it was called a cleansing diet.

This was on the fourth day. Joseph said to expect a less severe repetition of the same event a day or two later, and he was right. I had to make another dash for the toilet on the fifth day, but that was the end of it. Something else happened on the fifth day. I noticed my skin condition had cleared up. It disappeared then and has never returned.

Something else happened on the fifth day. I noticed my skin condition had cleared up. It has never returned.

I returned home to Canberra on the ninth day, which was the day we had to move on to the second stage of the diet. I did not feel I needed a solid meal, but I wanted one. It was a psychological thing—I had an urge to chew on something. That evening Joseph came to our house and helped us prepare our first solid meal in nine days. It was a pure vegetarian meal, of course, consisting of a range of vegetables.

For the next thirty-two days this was our

eating program: juice at breakfast, vegetable soup including solids at lunch, nuts and fresh juice in the afternoon, and a solid vegetarian meal at night. As before, I found it unexpectedly easy to stick to. Eventually the thirty-two days were up and our forty-day cleansing diet was over.

I felt supercharged, and it was a feeling that lasted right through the day.

How did I feel? Well, I can best describe it by saying I felt like jumping out of my skin. I experienced a sense of wellbeing I had not known before. Suddenly, I was needing only six hours' sleep a night; and when I did wake up I was wide awake and ready to go. I no longer felt that inertia in the morning that makes it so hard to drag oneself out of bed. I felt supercharged, and it was a feeling that lasted right through the day. At this time I was coming to Sydney for five days a week and returning to Canberra at weekends. Previously I had found this a wearing schedule, mentally and physically, but now I coasted through it.

I lost a lot of weight. When I started the diet I was about as heavy as I had ever been. I weighed a touch under fourteen stone, or about eighty-eight kilograms. On my kind of frame the extra weight may not have been obvious to others, but I could certainly feel it. I felt bloated, ponderous and generally unhealthy. Two months later I weighed just over twelve stone, or about seventy-eight kilograms. Judy lost weight, too. We worked out later that during this time we had both lost more than one ninth of our body weight. This was what Joseph Oros had told us to expect. When

I asked him about likely weight loss before we started the forty-day diet, he told me that my weight would fall until it reached the level it had been in my early twenties. This was precisely what happened.

New eating habits

The forty-day diet had a huge impact on our lives. It convinced Judy and me to become vegetarians. We both felt so good after it that neither of us had the slightest inclination to revert to our previous eating habits. We wanted to keep on feeling good.

The extra energy I felt had to be experienced to be believed. Later I discovered the reason for it. It wasn't simply that I was eating more nutritious food. My body was also no longer burdened with the task of digesting heavy meat-based meals. It has been said that you can run for ten kilometres on the energy it takes to digest a big meal. I well remember the effect that a three-course meal at night (usually followed by coffee and port) used to have on me when I ate out. I would wake up at three o'clock in the morning and lie there listening to my heart pounding and feeling distinctly on edge, as if my nerves were overloaded. In fact, unbeknown to me, my liver and kidneys were working frantically, too.

These were the signs of a body hard at work. My system was labouring to digest the huge quantity of animal protein and other protein I had eaten, and it was labouring to extract and expel (via the bladder) all the toxins contained in the meal. Hence the 3.00 a.m. urge to urinate.

I cannot vouch for the scientific accuracy of this observation, but I have been told the reason you often see tourist buses full of sleeping Japanese is that Japanese tourists in Australia tend to eat a lot of meat because it is relatively cheap here. As a result, their digestive systems are operating at full blast and their bodies are exhausted. I remember much the same happening on cricket trips when we travelled by bus. If we were in England and if we had stopped for a pub lunch of the usual meat-plus-potatoes variety, you could look around the bus in mid-afternoon and find nearly everyone asleep.

For four years after I became a pure vegetarian I worked long hours under pressure and drove up and down from Canberra repeatedly. If I had not changed my eating habits, if I were still filling myself with protein as before, I am sure I could not have survived those four years. In the event, I coped extremely well because I had the necessary energy.

> The forty-day diet is a cleansing diet. By the end of the forty days you will have rid yourself of many of the toxins and biological garbage that has been accumulating in your body for years. In fact, much of the cleansing occurs during the first eight days when you have nothing but liquids.

Liquid fasting is a science in itself. The theory behind it is simple. Whenever the body is starved of food, it begins to feed on itself; that is, to digest its own body tissue. Fortunately, it does this in a highly selective way by first digesting body tissues it can best do without; that is, those that are diseased, wasted or dying. So a liquid fast is like a spring clean.

You burn off the poisons and the rubbish.

A few days after starting the diet I developed a rash on my back. I am sure this was a manifestation of the fact that toxins in my body were being drawn out. A few weeks later the rash disappeared. It was the only negative effect I experienced during or after the diet.

Since then we have regained some of the weight we lost. As I write this, my weight is twelve stone twelve pounds, or not quite eighty-two kilograms. The main reason for the gain in weight is that, once the forty-day diet was over, the volume of food I was eating rose substantially. Also, I think that when you change your eating habits your body takes some time to adjust its metabolism to deal with the different kind and different volume of food.

As I said before, since becoming a vegetarian I have eaten only about a third of the volume of food that I ate before. Such a huge reduction in intake ought to have resulted, you would think, in a huge drop in weight; yet, as you see, I am only about a stone lighter. This says a good deal about the nutritional value of the food that I eat now.

As well as raising my energy level, the change in eating habits resulted in what I can only describe as a feeling of lightness. To put it another way, I no longer felt heavy and bloated for hours as I always did previously when I ate a sizeable meat-based meal. If I had one of these meals at night, I still felt heavy and bloated when I woke up. As a vegetarian, I can over-eat occasionally, but any feeling of discomfort that results from it always disappears within an hour or so. This is because the food I eat now is much easier for the body to digest. I certainly do not ever suffer from indigestion nowadays as I did regularly when I was eating meat.

To sum up, becoming a vegetarian made me feel brighter, lighter, more energetic, more alert. The next chapter will contain details of the forty-day diet—what to eat, when to eat it and how to prepare it.

CHAPTER TWENTY-FIVE
THE FORTY-DAY MENU

It is called a cleansing diet because it is meant to clean out the body. Its essential purpose is to reduce acidity and toxicity. It is a form of fasting, of course.

AS I HAVE SAID BEFORE, I do not suggest that everyone reading this book should consider going on the forty-day diet. Many people would not be physically or mentally capable of doing it. Others would find a diet of this kind impossible to stick to because of their personal circumstances. Those who are at least interested in having a go at it should read on, for in this chapter I will supply the details of the diet, just as Joseph Oros gave it to us.

Let me answer a few questions about the diet which you might wish to ask. Do I need superhuman strength of will to last the eight days on liquids, not to mention the thirty-two days that follow? The answer is no. I, for one, do not claim to possess that kind of willpower. What you need is not so much willpower as prior mental commitment to go through with it. You must make up your mind before you start that you really want to do it and that you will do it. If you get yourself into this frame of mind at the outset I am sure you will find the diet itself as easy to handle as I did.

Can I lead a normal, active life while on the diet? Speaking from my own experience, I can say definitely yes. You will have energy to spare. This was the most noticeable single effect the diet had on me. There is a simple explanation for this: the body is still getting the nutrients it needs from the liquids but it is not having to burn up energy digesting large quantities of food.

What does it all taste like? The broth on its own is bland, but you can add as much soya sauce as you like to give it a lift. The same is true of the herbal tea. The taste is fairly bland but can be sharpened by the ginseng. The vegetable soup, though, has quite a vibrant taste, thanks to the coconut milk, the fresh herbs, the sesame seeds, sunflower seeds and so on.

Here are the details of the forty-day diet:

EIGHT-DAY LIQUID CLEANSING DIET

It is called a cleansing diet because it is meant to clean out the body. Its essential purpose is to reduce acidity and toxicity. It is a form of fasting, of course, and like all fasts it has the effect of purifying the system by inducing the body to digest and so dispose of inferior cells. Like all fasts, too, it should not be attempted by anyone with reason to think it could harm them physically. If you are in any doubt about this, check with your health practitioner. Judy and I did the diet under supervision (Joseph

Oros was our 'supervisor'), which is the best way to do it.

The diet consists of four specific intakes of liquid each day—at breakfast, lunch, mid-afternoon and dinner. To help suppress feelings of hunger and to prevent the light-headed feeling people often experience while fasting, you are free to sip on a herbal tea mixture at any time during the day or evening. The operative word here is 'sip'. Do not gulp it down by the cupful; in fact, do not ever drink more than one third of a cup at a time.

The composition of this tea mixture is specific. Details of how to prepare the tea follow at the end of this section.

Breakfast

This consists of a mixed citrus fruit juice, squeezed from raw fruit. Each breakfast serving should consist of the juice from one small to medium grapefruit, one lemon, one lime, two oranges and two mandarins. Altogether, this should make one large glass. The juice should be lightly warmed before drinking, the reason being that the warming brings out the flavours and makes the juice easier for the body to absorb.

Lunch

Vegetable broth. You can drink as much as you like, but try to drink it as close to midday as possible. The broth is simple to prepare. Boil any mixture of fresh vegetables, such as carrots, pumpkins and beans, and keep boiling until the vegetables have been softened. Then pour off the liquid, or, rather, the broth, into a cup or mug. There are two special things to be added to it before you drink it: one teaspoon of honey and a dash of sugar-free soy sauce or salt-reduced Tamari (Spiral brand). *Do not throw out the vegetables.* They can be blended and frozen for use as a base for dips or sauces when you move on to the solid diet.

Afternoon juice

Take a Granny Smith or Jonathan apple and cut it into eighths. Put the apple through a juicer with the following:

one small carrot
small piece of turnip
small piece of parsnip
one celery stick
small piece of celeriac
small piece of swede
piece of cucumber
one small squash
some cauliflower and broccoli

Warm slightly in a saucepan over a low heat. Sip slowly.

Dinner

Vegetable broth as prepared for lunch.

Herbal tea mixture

You need two pieces of equipment for this: a narrow-necked vacuum flask (we use a 750 ml flask) and an infuser, preferably of the cloth (not metal!)

type. As an alternative, you can use a porcelain or pottery teapot with a shorter infusion time—say, three minutes.

Two types of herbal tea are suitable: Roha Sedative-Stress Herbal Tea or Herba-Heal No. 4 Herbal Tea. There are three other ingredients:

Swedish bitters (Dr Theiss brand)
honey or black sugar
pure concentrated ginseng extract (Il Hwa brand)

(All these ingredients can be bought at health food shops.)

To prepare the tea, place two large teaspoons of tea in the infuser, which is then placed in the neck of the vacuum flask. Boil some water and pour it into the flask through the infuser. Place the screw top on the infusion bag in the flask, pressing it in firmly to prevent heat escaping, and allow the tea to draw for ten to fifteen minutes. Take the screw top off the flask, remove the infuser and add about one teaspoon of honey or black sugar per cup. The quantity can be varied, depending on how you want the tea to taste. Also add one teaspoon of Swedish bitters per cup and add one measure of ginseng concentrate to the flask. Use the measure that comes with the concentrate when you buy it. Omit the bitters, though, if you are taking herbal remedies, because the bitters can affect their performance.

Having been introduced to this herbal tea when I did the diet, I soon formed a habit of sipping on it. It is refreshing, it gives me energy, and it prevents me feeling hungry between meals. If I have any tea left over at the end of the day, I keep the flask beside my bed and sip from it if I wake during the night.

One-month cleansing diet

This thirty-two-day diet follows immediately after the eight-day diet. It is meant to finish off the cleansing program which the eight-day diet began. The diet consists of three meals plus an afternoon snack, but feel free to drink fresh juices when you feel like it and to sip on the herbal tea mixture previously described. If for whatever reason you have to resort to buying juice, make sure you choose brands which contain no added sugar.

Breakfast

Mixed citrus juice as in the eight-day program.

Lunch

'Joseph's Vegetable Soup', so named because it was Joseph Oros who gave us the recipe. There is a reasonably long list of ingredients, but make sure you include them all, for each is a necessary part of the whole. The ingredients are:

one or more vegetables of your choice (carrot, pumpkin, cauliflower, beans, peas or whatever)
soy sauce or tamari
coconut milk
fresh herbs (mint, parsley, coriander)
sunflower seeds
sesame seeds

nori (Japanese seaweed sheets)

Hungarian paprika

soy cheese

The last of these should be added after blending the rest.

Boil the vegetable or vegetables in water until they are soft. The quantity of vegetables and water you use obviously depends on how many servings are needed. As a guide, I suggest that for one person you should boil the equivalent of three to four cups of vegetables in two to three cups of water. You can vary this ratio depending on whether you prefer the soup watery or thick.

While the vegetables are boiling, add the other ingredients to a blender in the following order and amounts: two dessertspoons of soy or tamari per serve, a quarter to half a cup of coconut milk per serve, a handful of fresh herbs per serve, half a cup each of sesame seeds and sunflower seeds per serve, a quarter to half a strip of nori per serve depending on the size, and one teaspoon of Hungarian paprika per serve.

Blend these with the vegetables in a blender until liquefied. Add some slivers of soy cheese when serving if desired.

Afternoon snack

Nibble on raw nuts—almonds, walnuts, sunflower seeds, pinenuts and pistachios—and drink 'afternoon juice' as prepared for the eight-day diet.

Dinner

This must be a vegan meal; that is, a meal entirely free of all animal products, including dairy foods and eggs. Instead, eat foods such as lentils, tofu, tempeh, chickpeas and red kidney beans for protein. Cook with no oil except sesame oil. Fresh onion and garlic are fine if required but do not cook them because they give off ascetic acid. Asafoetida powder can be used to simulate an onion taste if required.

CHAPTER TWENTY-SIX

ANTIOXIDANT SUPPLEMENTS

The free radical versus antioxidant concept is at the vanguard of current medical research, but already it has a large body of expert opinion behind it.

ONE OF THE MOST important developments in medical science in the closing years of the twentieth century has been the recognition that the presence in the body of chemical particles called 'free radicals' has an absolutely profound effect on our health; indeed, some scientists are convinced that free radicals are actually the main cause of many common diseases as well as a key factor in the aging process.

That is the bad news. The good news is that the harmful effects of free radicals can largely be nullified by chemical agents known as antioxidants. In other words, if the body has a big enough supply of antioxidants, the diseases can be avoided and aging can be slowed.

The terms 'free radicals' and 'antioxidants' are still confusing to most people, and I partly blame the terms themselves for that, for they sound as if they belong in a chemistry laboratory. Still, they are the terms we are stuck with, and it is important than we understand what they stand for.

So for millions of years the forces of good (antioxidants) provided a natural protection against the forces of evil (free radicals).

Free radicals are electrically charged molecules. They are extremely potent chemically, and as they wander about the body they produce chemical reactions which damage cells and cause disease. If all this sounds new to you, it is because it *is* new. The free radical versus antioxidant concept is at the vanguard of current medical research, but already it has a large body of expert opinion behind it. I referred in Chapter 20 to Dr Ken Cooper's book *The Antioxidant Revolution*. The fact he chose to use the word 'revolution' in the title indicates the impact the concept is making.

Free radicals come from two sources. Some are created within the body itself as part of normal body chemistry. Specifically, these free radicals are a by-product of the chemical reaction taking place inside the body's cells that enables us to convert the food we eat into energy. This chemical reaction is called oxidation.

The second source of free radicals is the environment. We absorb free radicals from cigarette smoke, from traces of pesticides on the fruit and vegetables we eat, from exhaust and other air pollution, from household chemicals, from preservatives in food, from X-rays, from ultraviolet sunlight.

The production of free radicals within the body has been happening since time began, so the body is accustomed to the problem and knows how to deal with it. The way it deals with it is by neutralising the free radicals with antioxidants. Like free radicals, antioxidants come from two sources. One is internal (these antioxidants are produced within the body) and other external. The external source is simply the food we eat. Three vitamins—A, C and E—have an antioxidant effect. So does the mineral selenium.

So for millions of years the forces of good (antioxidants) provided a natural protection against the forces of evil (free radicals). In other words, a kind of natural balance existed between the two. Over the past 200 years or so, mainly in Western society this balance has been increasingly upset. On the one hand, our intake of free radicals from an increasingly contaminated environment is greater than it was. I have heard one medical expert suggest that we ingest a million free radicals each time we take a deep breath. On the other hand, our intake of antioxidants in the food we eat is less than it was. Clearly, there is an imbalance here which must be a danger to our health.

Why good food is not enough

It has been estimated that 90 per cent of the antioxidants that occur naturally in food are destroyed by the time the food is processed, packaged and stacked on the supermarket shelves. People who are aware of the problem do their best to counter it by buying mainly fresh food, but even if the food is both fresh and organically grown this cannot make up the shortfall. The plain yet alarming fact is that it is virtually impossible today to obtain all the nutrients you need for good health (vitamins, antioxidants, minerals) from the food you eat.

It has been estimated that 90 per cent of the antioxidants that occur naturally in food are destroyed by the time the food is processed.

There is an explanation for this. Nowadays, fruit and vegetables are routinely harvested before they ripen to ensure they look their best in the shops. (Having owned a mango plantation, I personally know this to be true.) Many of the nutrients in food are formed just before ripening, which means they are missing from the prematurely harvested fresh food we buy in the shops. So fresh food is lower in antioxidants and vitamins than it used to be and than it should be. Packaged food and processed food are even worse in this respect, for few antioxidants survive the manufacturing process, especially if the food is subjected to extreme heat.

The deficiency in minerals has a separate explanation. The farmlands where our food is grown tend to be low in minerals, which means that the plants that grow on them and the animals that graze on them must also be heavily depleted in minerals. More will be said about this in Chapter 27.

In the light of all this, it is reasonable to argue that although men of my father's and grandfather's generations may have consumed even more fatty foods than men of the same age today—red meat, cheese,

There is still much to be discovered about everyday sources of free radicals.

bacon, eggs, chips, butter, ice-cream—their nutrition was probably better than ours if only because their food was more nutritious. The vegetables and fruit they ate would certainly have been more nutritious than the modern product. Many of their vegetables were grown in the backyard, and they would have been eaten as soon as they were ripe.

There is still much to be discovered about everyday sources of free radicals. The modern environment may be a more potent source of them than anyone yet realises. Recently I talked to a man who used to sing on the club circuit in Sydney. Before appearing at a leagues club one evening, he stepped onto a small verandah outside his dressing room to do his usual pre-performance breathing exercises and noticed fumes being pumped out from a vent in a nearby wall. A club employee happened to come into the dressing-room, so he asked him about it. The employee replied, 'That's just the air being sucked out of the room where you'll be performing.' The singer was horrified. Just being in the room would be bad enough, he thought, but to have to perform in it was many times worse, since he necessarily had to take in deep breaths while singing. It occurred to him that he must be breathing huge volumes of fumes at every club that he sang at.

The thought of this was so appalling that he gave up singing for good, moved to Queensland and is today growing avocados there. He felt instinctively that filling his lungs with smoke and fumes must be unhealthy. Although he did not realise it at the time, by quitting the club circuit he was really sparing himself severe free-radical damage. The quantity of free radicals he sucked in every time he sang a song can only be guessed at.

> In a situation where there are more free radicals to attack our bodies and fewer antioxidants to combat them, the obvious way to redress the balance and protect our health is by taking antioxidants in the form of natural food supplements. This is particularly important for the middle-aged, given that the natural production of antioxidants within our bodies seems to fall off sharply as we get older.

Antioxidants are normally taken in the form of vitamin supplements and are available from several sources, including health stores. Personally, I am convinced that the richest single source of antioxidants is a group of compounds that has both amazing properties and a complicated name: *oligomeric-proanthocyanidins.* They are known as OPCs for short. I have heard an American doctor predict that OPCs will one day be regarded as the health miracle of the 1990s. Their antioxidant effect is said to be twenty times more powerful than vitamin C and fifty times more powerful than vitamin E. OPCs are natural extracts from highly specific plant sources, the most common of them being grape seeds and the bark of a tree native to North America, the maritime pine tree. Extracts from both of these are present in several of the antioxidant products now on the market.

THE FREE-RADICAL THREAT

Antioxidants get their name from the fact that they counter the effects of oxidation in the body. Oxidation is a very common chemical reaction in nature, a familiar example of it being the rusting of metal exposed to air. Here is another example. Cut an apple and leave the cut surface exposed. Within ten minutes the surface will start to brown off, almost as if it were rusting. What we are seeing is the effect of oxidation. Free radicals produced by the oxidation are attacking and damaging the apple's cells. On the other hand, if you squeeze fresh lemon juice over the cut apple the exposed surface will not go brown, the reason being that the juice is rich in antioxidants.

Doctors now believe that free-radical damage may be a key factor in as many as sixty diseases and conditions, among them cancer, arthritis, diabetes and premature aging. There is also growing evidence to suggest that oxidation is a leading cause of arteriosclerosis which, in turn, is a leading cause of heart attacks. The Heart Research Institute in Sydney has based a lot of its current work on this thesis. The theory is that if oxidation can be reduced, heart disease will be reduced, too.

In the light of all this, I find the argument for taking antioxidant and vitamin supplements irresistible. Some products on the market now contain a combination of the main antioxidant ingredients—vitamin C, vitamin E and betacarotene (which is converted into vitamin A in the body). Incidentally, the reason we take betacarotene instead of vitamin A is that vitamin A itself can be toxic when taken in large doses.

As well as taking antioxidant supplements, you should try to ensure that the food you eat is as rich in antioxidants as possible. Eat as much fresh food as possible, especially citrus fruit and green leafy vegetables. Cooking of any kind destroys antioxidants, but, if you have a choice, steam your food rather than baking or even boiling it.

More information on antioxidants is available on my web site, Greg Chappell's World. The address is www.greg-chappell.com.au.

CHAPTER TWENTY-SEVEN
MINERAL SUPPLEMENTS

...the cost of taking mineral supplements, usually a few dollars a day, is negligible compared with the potential they offer for maintaining good health.

TODAY, TWENTY YEARS after I began my search for a healthier lifestyle, I am convinced that the foods which make up my diet are the healthiest available. The fruit, vegetables, grain foods (pasta, breads, rice) and honey that my wife and I eat are the best and freshest we can find. For the most part, they are organically grown. Yet this diet of ours is by no means complete. In particular, it almost certainly lacks vital minerals.

There is a scientific background to this which I touched on in Chapter 26. It will be familiar to anyone who has looked into the matter of mineral supplements. In the United States and many others parts of the world, the modern practice of intensive farming is at the centre of it all. Soils have generally become so depleted of minerals in the past thirty years or more that the plants grown in them are necessarily lacking in minerals, too. Plants do not make minerals. All they do is extract minerals from the soil—assuming there are minerals left to extract; in fact, farmlands around the world, including Australia, are deficient in them. There are not enough of some minerals and a total absence of others.

In Australia, the problem is not only intensive farming but the extreme age of our soils. Australian soils are among the oldest in the world, dating back hundreds of thousands of years. By comparison, American soils are still in their infancy. They are glaciated soils and therefore under 10 000 years old. Australian soils are generally low in key nutrients such as calcium and magnesium. Certain Australian soils, including many granite soils, are also low in vital trace minerals such as selenium. The upshot is we are obliged to look beyond the food we eat for the nutrients we need. This is why we take mineral supplements.

The textbooks tell us that we need about ninety nutrients a day—sixty minerals, sixteen vitamins, twelve essential amino acids and three essential fatty acids—to maintain good health. If we are missing out on any of these, we will suffer a deficiency which is bound to lead to an illness of some sort. It may take forty years to show up, but it will show up.

It would be possible to fill twenty more pages by listing the illnesses that can be traced back to some deficiency in minerals. Calcium deficiency alone is said to be the cause of 147 different complaints. Predictably, many of the illnesses resulting from mineral deficiencies show up in middle age—illnesses such as kidney stones, arthritis, aneurisms, high blood pressure, prostate trouble, eczema and anaemia. Cancer, too, is being linked increasingly to a lack of specific minerals, one of them being selenium. It is not surprising, therefore, to learn that those few odd places around the world where people are renowned for

Plants do not make minerals. All they do is extract minerals from the soil—assuming there are minerals left to extract.

living to a great age also happen to be places where the soils are rich in minerals.

I once received a personal lesson in the importance of minerals in the diet. In 1979 I was diagnosed as having a complaint with the rather grim title of Bell's palsy. It is essentially a neurological disorder which results in one side of the face becoming paralysed to a greater or lesser degree. It caused me to miss a vital World Series Cricket 'Super Test' that year. One of my eyes would not close completely, and the team doctor refused to let me play for fear of dirt or grit getting into the eye and causing more problems.

Calcium deficiency (as I now know) is a main cause of Bell's palsy, and research has shown that, contrary to popular opinion, calcium deficiency can be caused by an excessive intake of dairy foods. One explanation of this, which I find plausible, is that by eating protein-rich dairy foods you can end up with a surplus of proteins in the system, which makes the blood more acidic. The body cannot tolerate this, and will do whatever is necessary to keep the blood's pH level in balance. What it does do, in fact, is leach calcium out of the bones and other parts of the body, thus producing a calcium deficiency. Another factor, which I have mentioned previously, is the level of phosphorous in the body. High levels of phosphorus cause calcium to be leached from the body. Animal protein—meat and dairy products—are rich in phosphorus. In my own case, the Bell's palsy disappeared after I gave up dairy foods.

An American doctor named Joel Wallach has thrown an intriguing new light on the twin subjects of minerals and nutrition. Wallach's background is in farming. Having grown up on a farm, he became an agricultural scientist and then a vet. Finally, he became a naturopathic doctor. The point he makes, which as a city-bred person I find fascinating, is that farmers routinely supply their cattle with mineral supplements to keep them healthy yet rarely give their own children mineral supplements. In other words, veterinary scientists recognised long ago that illnesses on the farm can often be traced back to a nutritional deficiency, which in most cases means a mineral deficiency.

By contrast, many doctors tend to ignore nutrition. They habitually approach illnesses from the opposite direction and treat ailments with drugs. Even a few dietitians tend to ignore nutrition. I have already made it clear I am not in favour of recommending detailed diets that people are supposed to follow slavishly, meal by meal. The trouble with these diets is that they cannot possibly suit the needs and circumstances of the individual. Worse, there is reason to believe that some of the more way-out diets may be deficient nutritionally. In particular, they may lack one or more of the essential minerals we have just been looking at and so leave the people who are following the diets exposed to illness.

Supplements: do we need them?

Let us accept that minerals are important to health. The question then arises: should middle-aged men without any pronounced symptoms of illness which might be traced back to a mineral deficiency bother taking mineral supplements?

My strong opinion is that, yes, they would be very wise to take them if only as a preventative measure. Not all medical experts would agree with this. Some scoff at the idea of nutritional supplements, saying they are unnecessary and a waste of money. All that supplements produce, they say, is expensive urine. My response to this is that the cost of taking mineral supplements, usually a few dollars a day, is negligible compared with the potential they offer for maintaining good health. It is a financial risk worth running. It is the other risk, the risk of contracting some disease because of a mineral deficiency in my food, that worries me more.

This is consistent with the general philosophy of being proactive in matters of health. In the battle against disease, we need to strike the first blow. Our bodies are under constant stress, and we need to take steps to protect them. Talk about stress these days and people assume you are talking about mental stress. There is another type of stress which is not so well recognised—physical stress. Gardeners speak of their plants as being under stress from the heat, or wind, or dry conditions. Similarly, our bodies are under stress from pollution, radiation, chemicals of all kinds. We need to be aware of this and be thinking all the time of how we can protect ourselves.

The next question is: given that there are as many as sixty minerals which must be obtained from some source every day, how can the middle-aged man without any specific symptoms possibly choose which minerals to take? In my view, he should take the lot. If you visit your local health store you will find a number of supplement products which contain traces of all the minerals you need. Again, there is every chance you will not need most of them, but by taking these products you are effectively protecting your health with comprehensive insurance.

My personal view is that minerals in liquid form, sometimes known as colloidal minerals, are the most sensible choice, for they are more easily absorbed by the body. Solid mineral supplements in pill or powder form are hard to digest and will often pass straight through the body. These colloidal minerals can be bought at most health stores or through independent nutritional supplement suppliers who deliver direct.

As with antioxidants, further information on mineral supplements may be obtained from my website, Greg Chappell's World (www.gregchappell.com.au).

CHAPTER TWENTY-EIGHT
DANGEROUS PURSUITS

...basically all that the experts have managed to discover is that we should not smoke, that we should eat more fruit and vegetables and that we should exercise regularly.

AFTER ALL THE BILLIONS of dollars that have been spent on health research in the twentieth century, basically all that the experts have managed to discover is that we should not smoke, that we should eat more fruit and vegetables and that we should exercise regularly. They are three lessons which ought to be familiar to us all. I find it hard to believe that anyone who heeds the last two would not heed the first. People who care enough about their health to go out of their way to eat nutritional foods and exercise could hardly be smokers, too. Or could they?

Those of us who are middle-aged today grew up at a time when smoking was frowned upon by the medical profession but was certainly not identified as being viciously destructive of health. Most of us smoked then and, happily, most of us have given it up since. According to statistics supplied by the Quit Campaign, 72 per cent of men smoked in 1972. Today, the figure is not much more than 20 per cent.

When I started playing cricket nearly everyone smoked. There was little awareness of the danger of smoking.

So much has been written about how to stop smoking that I would not attempt to add to it here except to say again that you will certainly find smoking easier to give up if you change the way you think about it. A friend told me with pride the other day that he had just celebrated an important anniversary. It was twenty-five years, he said, since he stubbed out his last cigarette. I asked him how he managed to resist the temptation to smoke. He said he used a simple mental device he invented himself: every time he felt like smoking he would try to remember as vividly as he could all the bad things about cigarettes—the foul taste they produced in his mouth, the dizziness he experienced whenever he lit one up early in the morning, the headache he suffered when he smoked too many, the distaste he always felt for the clouds of smoke he was producing, the stale smell the smoke left in his office.

In other words, he had deliberately changed the way he thought about smoking. The method worked. He was twenty-nine years old then and he had been smoking twenty to thirty cigarettes a day since he was eighteen. He gave smoking up at one stroke, cold turkey. I am not sure everyone can do it this way. A fifty-cigarettes-a-day man might find it impossible to give up all fifty at once. If this is impossible, then by all means try to do it by cutting back gradually. Set yourself targets. Limit yourself to forty a day for the first week, thirty for the next and so on until you quit altogether. Don't drag the process out too long though, lest you lose your initial resolve.

When I started playing cricket nearly everyone smoked. There was little awareness of the danger of smoking and absolutely no awareness of the danger of passive smoking. In every players' room there was a permanent haze of cigarette smoke, and I am sure I experienced the equivalent of a lifetime of smoking merely by sitting in those rooms over a period of nearly twenty years. In fact, when I first made the Australian team I was one of the few players who did not smoke. I did not like breathing in and smelling other people's smoke, but I put up with it because it was the norm. In any case, with Doug Walters in the dressing-room, we hardly needed to do our own smoking.

I tried smoking myself on a few occasions, but fortunately I did not like it. I am sure I did not ever do the drawback. My brother Ian used to smoke. Luckily for him, he contracted pleurisy in his mid-twenties and was told by his doctor to stop smoking for a few weeks while he recovered. After he had done so, he decided not to take it up again. Many men in my experience have given up smoking in similar circumstances.

DRINKING: HOW MANY A DAY?

Drinking is another matter again. Few of us either wish to or need to give up drinking altogether. Many of us, though, would like to cut down on how much we drink. There are certainly quite a few of us ('us' being middle-aged men) who need to cut down for our own sake. Surveys of Australians as a whole show consistently that the heaviest drinkers in the land are men in the age range thirty to sixty-five. Men in their twenties may break out regularly and drink huge quantities of booze in one night, but the statistics show they do not drink as consistently as older men do and so do not consume as much over a period. In fact, as many as 10 per cent of adult males between the ages of thirty and forty-five consume alcohol to an extent that is dangerous to their health. Men over sixty-five drink less than middle-aged men do, but they drink even more consistently. In fact, almost a third of men in this age bracket drink on six or seven days a week.

Surveys of Australians as a whole show consistently that the heaviest drinkers in the land are men in the age range thirty to sixty-five.

For some years now it has been accepted by medical authorities everywhere that a modest amount of booze is beneficial to your health, that, in the words of the old music hall song, 'a little of what you fancy does you good'. But how much is modest? In 1997 the *British Medical Journal* published the results of an interesting survey on the matter. A total of 12000 doctors in Britain, middle-aged and older, were studied over a thirteen-year period, and it was found that the death rate was lowest in those who averaged two to three drinks a day.

Jill Margo wrote about this in the *Weekend Australian* newspaper and spoke to an Australian expert on the subject, Professor John Saunders of the University of Queensland. His view was that drinking delivered the peak health benefit when the rate of consumption was two drinks a day. Drinking at this level helped to prevent the arteries becoming clogged, it helped to prevent blood clots being formed and might even help to break down existing clots, and it provided some protection against high blood pressure and other conditions.

Diabetes: a lifestyle disease

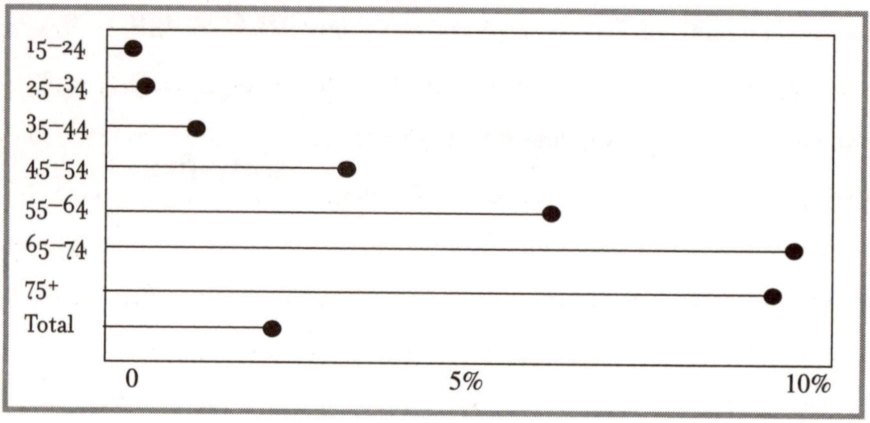

In middle-aged men diabetes tends to be a lifestyle disease. It is often linked with excessive drinking and poor nutrition. This chart shows the percentage of men in each of the various age groups who have diabetes. It illustrates how the incidence of the disease increases rapidly when men move into middle age. (Source: Australian Bureau of Statistics)

For all these reasons, moderate drinking does reduce the risk of coronary disease. According to Professor Saunders, if you average one or two drinks a day you are 30 to 50 per cent less likely to develop heart disease than if you are a teetotaller. Once you exceed three drinks a day, however, the booze begins to have a damaging effect. The message, then, is: drink one, two or even three a day with a clear conscience but do not drink four or more.

Notwithstanding all the benefits to be gained from moderate drinking, Professor Saunders told Jill Margo he would not advise someone who hardly drank at all to start having two drinks a day. The worry was they might end up drinking more than that. Then Professor Saunders made an extremely important point. There were other ways, he said, to reduce the risk of heart disease, most notably by exercising, improving your diet and, of course, giving up cigarettes. To take this point further, it would be foolish in the extreme for a middle-aged man to rely on a couple of drinks a day to protect his health and ignore the need to exercise and eat nutritious food. There could hardly be a falser sense of security than that.

CHAPTER TWENTY-NINE
A FEW FAVOURITE DISHES

PEOPLE WHO ARE THINKING of cutting down on their meat are usually keen to have some appetising vegetarian meals recommended to them. Taste is entirely a matter of individual preference, yet I am happy to nominate the vegetarian dishes that I enjoy myself. A list of six follows. Try them by all means. I hope you enjoy them as much as I do.

VEGETARIAN SHEPHERD'S PIE

Shepherd's pie was a favourite of mine when I ate meat, and it is still a favourite of mine in its vegetarian form. The dish can be made to complement the rest of your dinner menu or to be served on its own, perhaps preceded by a compatible soup. By varying the ingredients, you can prepare it in a number of ethnic styles, three of which – Italian, Indian and traditional Australian – are described here.

The base

The base of the pie can consist of any of the following – lentils, dried beans, split peas, chickpeas or vegetables – which therefore take on the role normally filled by minced lamb.

If lentils or chick peas are your preferred base, you must soak them overnight and then rinse. If you are cooking for, say, a family of four, you would need two to three cups of the pulses (lentils, beans, chick peas) or five to six cups of the vegetables (say, broccoli, carrot, cauliflower, sweet potato). If you wanted a base of both pulses and vegetables, you might use one and a half to two cups of the former and three to four cups of the latter. Simmer your choice of base in water seasoned with whole black peppercorns, caraway seeds and a few dried bay leaves. You will find a most delicious aroma pervades your kitchen.

The top layer

The top layer of the dish can be made from rice, polenta or potatoes, depending on which style of pie you have opted for. Here is a guide to quantities based on a family of four:

For a rice top, use two to two and a half cups of uncooked rice.

For a polenta top, add one and a half to two cups of dry polenta to three to four cups of water and bring to the boil. Then lower the heat and continue stirring all the time to prevent lumping. As you do so, keep a lid over the pan and spoon, because the polenta mixture does tend to spit.

For a potato top, use five medium potatoes — or five large potatoes, if appetites are big. I suggest you mash the potatoes with either Herbamare (herb salt from the wholefood shop) and soya milk or salt, soya milk and a few slurps of a good olive oil. Nuttelex, a dairy-free margarine, may be used instead of the olive oil.

Whichever kind of top you choose, you can cook it in the same way as the base, again resulting in a delicious flavour.

Finally, place the two layers in an oven-proof dish, adding the various additions, as described below, for the ethnic style you prefer, and finally brown in the oven.

Italian-style

The usual choice here is a base made of dried beans and a top of polenta.

Pop some fresh, torn basil leaves into a casserole dish.

Mix the cooked base mixture with some toasted pine nuts, a little tomato puree and Herbamare (herb salt from the wholefood shop) and place it on top of the basil leaves.

Top the lot with dollops of cooked, seasoned polenta. After warming it in the oven (don't overheat), serve topped with fresh, whole basil leaves.

If an onion or garlicky flavour is preferred, I suggest using a substitute, asafoetida, a very pungent yellow powder derived from the gum of certain plants. Only a small amount is needed (a teaspoonful perhaps) and can be added to the base mixture before heating.

Indian-style

Here, the base can be of lentils, chick peas, split peas or vegetables, and the top is normally of rice.

Add a teaspoonful each of cardamom, garam masala, cumin powder, turmeric or coriander, chilli and asafoetida if desired, to coconut cream (half to one cup) and add to the base mixture.

Also, add a little salt for seasoning. This produces the effect of dhal when lentils or split peas are used.

Top with boiled rice and serve garnished with fresh coriander leaves, pappadams, chutney and cucumber raita.

Cucumber raita consists of chopped cucumber in thick yoghurt plus a little salt, pepper, lemon juice and fresh-chopped herbs, preferably dill, parsley, coriander and a few black mustard seeds.

Australian-style

Vegetables and/or split peas are the preferred base and mashed potato the top, seasoned with either a variety of herbs — tarragon, marjoram or sage.

We always keep a little of the water that was used to boil the vegetables or pulses and, having thickened it with cornflower, arrowroot or a small amount of coconut cream, add it to the vegetable or pulse mixture.

A final tip: sprinkle some paprika on the mashed potato and top with fresh sage leaves.

Chickpea curry

Curries are a favourite meal in our home, and this is probably my favourite curry. The chickpeas give it a distinctive flavour, which may be the reason for its special appeal. We obtained the following recipe straight out of the Squirrels' *Best Of One And Two* vegetarian cookbook. I recommend the book to anyone wanting to try a range of vegetarian meals.

Ingredients

(Our own preference is for a tablespoon of asafoetida instead of the onions and garlic.)

200 g chickpeas
3 onions, chopped
4 cloves garlic, crushed
a small piece of ginger, grated
2 tablespoons cumin
1 tablespoon coriander
2 tablespoons turmeric
1 tablespoon paprika
1/2 tablespoon chilli
2 tablespoons sweet mango chutney
2 potatoes, cut in chunks
100 grams green beans, chopped
1 small eggplant, cubed
4 tablespoons cold-pressed olive oil
salt

Method

Step one: Soak the chickpeas overnight in plenty of water. Next day boil for an hour or so until very tender.

Step two: Meanwhile, heat the oil in a pan and fry the onions, garlic and ginger gently for ten minutes – or less if onions are omitted. Add the spices and fry for two minutes. Then add two cups of water.

Step three: Add the vegetables, season well with salt (Herbamare) and simmer for half an hour until tender.

Step four: Add the chickpeas and chutney and cook gently for ten minutes.

Step five: Serve the curry with rice and traditional accompaniments – yoghurt (soy), pappadams, chutneys, coconut and bananas. (These last two, coconut and bananas, seem to be western additions to curries. The Indians do not use them in this way.)

Laksa

Laksa is essentially a curry soup with rice noodles. It is a Malaysian dish, yet it seems to be a staple meal in many Asian countries. It can be served as a soup, starter or as a main meal. The following version is my favourite, but you can make it spicier if you prefer.

Ingredients

3 tablespoons olive or sesame oil

1 teaspoon asafoetida powder or 1 onion and 2 garlic cloves, crushed until transparent

2/3 whole chilli or similar portion of chilli powder

1 dessertspoon turmeric

1 dessertspoon coriander

2 tablespoons lemon rind

1 teaspoon Laos powder (optional)

Brazil or macadamia nut kernels (optional)

8 cups vegetable stock

1/2 block coconut cream

2 teaspoons black sugar

a pinch of salt

1 large handful of stringless beans (five to seven cm in length)

1 cup chopped tomato

1 cup tofu, cut into large cubes (available from good health food shops and supermarkets)

1 packet vermicelli (rice) noodles

2 cups bean sprouts

3 small cucumbers, coarsely chopped

fresh mint

3 shallots, chopped

Method

Step one: Prepare vermicelli noodles according to instructions on packet.

Step two: In a large, heavy saucepan, combine oil, chilli, spices and nuts and saute for approximately five minutes.

Step three: Add the stock, coconut cream, sugar, salt, beans, tomatoes and tofu. Reduce heat and simmer, covered, for ten to fifteen minutes, stirring occasionally to prevent curdling.

Step four: Meanwhile, arrange separate quantities of noodles, bean sprouts, cucumber, mint and chopped shallots in individual serving bowls (about two-thirds full). Pour the soup over and serve immediately.

NOTE: The amounts mentioned above are not to be followed to the gram. Play around with the quantities—especially the chilli!—until you have a combination of flavours you like.

When cooking for a 'mixed diet' family, cook the laksa as described, then pour the required quantity of the soup (well stirred) into a separate saucepan, add slivers or cubes of meat or seafood and cook gently: a few minutes for seafood and ten to fifteen minutes for meat.

Mixed vegetable pasta

This is a standard, country-style Italian-based dish and can be varied to suit your own taste; for instance, you can add one, two or more vegetables of your own choice. Match it with the pasta of your choice. My own preference is for egg-free spaghetti.

Ingredients

1 tablespoon olive oil

1 teaspoon asafoetida powder

a large pinch each of dried sage, basil, tarragon

fresh herbs of your choice such as parsley, basil, rosemary (change the combination to suit taste and availability)

a little herb salt

pepper

small sprinkle of fresh or dried chopped chillies (optional)

2–3 cups mixed chopped vegetables: zucchini, eggplant, capsicum, beans, etc (experiment with different combinations)

1 tin tomatoes (400 g)

Method

Step one: Saute spices and fresh/dried herbs for roughly three to five minutes to bring out the flavours, then add the vegetables.

Step two: Stir to coat all the vegetables and saute for a few more minutes before adding the tinned tomatoes in their own juice.

Step three: Meanwhile, cook up the pasta of your choice. Try grains other than wheat and preferably use pasta that is egg free. Drain and rinse with cold water to stop the cooking process and coat with some sauce. Serve in a bowl and top with sauce and vegetables. Sprinkle with herbs for the believers and parmesan for the non-believers.

NOTE: I usually cook up, in a pressure cooker, tomatoes I buy cheaply from my greengrocer because they are slightly damaged and can't be sold, adding whole peppercorns, bay leaves and caraway seeds, then pureeing. Excess tomato sauce can be frozen in containers for later use.

Hunza pie

This dish takes its name from the ancient mountain kingdom of Hunza, now part of Pakistan, whose people are said to be the healthiest in the world and regularly live to an age of 100 or more. Even today, disease is said to be virtually unknown there, one explanation being that the Hunza people both drink and irrigate their crops with glacial water rich in minerals. The pie is, of course, a vegetable pie, and the recipe provided here is for a slightly curried version of it. If you prefer, you can replace the curry powder with your own choice of spices.

Ingredients

For the filling:

2 tablespoons oil

4 cups diced vegetables (carrots, leeks, celery, cauliflower, broccoli, beans, pumpkin, courgettes, etc)

2–4 teaspoons curry powder

2 cloves crushed garlic

1 400 g can crushed tomatoes

freshly ground black pepper

2–3 tablespoons crunchy peanut butter

2–3 tablespoons soy yoghurt

1 cup puffed wheat

cubes of tofu (optional)

For the pastry:

1 1/2 cups flour

sprinkle of sea salt

1–2 teaspoons ground coriander

1 small can (300 g) butter beans

1/2 cup margarine (optional)

water as needed.

Method

Step one: Heat the oil and saute the vegetables until tender. Add curry powder, garlic and tomatoes. Cover and simmer for fifteen minutes.

Step two: Season to taste and add peanut butter and yoghurt. Transfer to a casserole dish, cover, cool and refrigerate overnight. (You can omit the overnight refrigeration if you don't have time, but it improves the taste.)

Step three: Mix flour, coriander and butter beans. Add melted margarine (or just rub in) and enough water to make a thick dough. Shape dough into a thick top for your casserole dish.

Step four: Add puffed wheat to the vegetable mix and cover with the pastry top. (The puffed wheat bulks up the mixture.)

Step five: Bake at 190°C for about thirty minutes.

Chargrilled Vegetable or Tofu Lasagne

One advantage of this meal is that both meat and vegetarian versions of it can be prepared quite easily at the one time, which makes it possible to please everyone in the family. In fact, it is really a three-in-one meal. It can be based on steamed vegetables, chargrilled vegetables or minced meat. It is one of the latest additions to our home menu, and it is already a favourite of mine.

Ingredients

cold-pressed extra virgin olive oil or linseed or sesame oil

1 large eggplant, sliced thickly

2 capsicums, quartered and seeds removed

1 sweet potato, sliced thickly

several large field mushrooms, stems removed

small block tofu (optional)

1 teaspoon dried basil

cracked black pepper

herb salt to taste

2–3 tablespoons flour (cornmeal or polenta flour is good)

salt and pepper

freshly ground nutmeg

3–4 cups soya milk

3 cups tomato puree or fresh tomato sauce

soya cheese slices

Method

Step one: In a large bowl, coat the vegetables with the oil, dried basil, herb salt and cracked pepper.

Step two: Place the mixture on a baking tray and bake at 190–200°C for twenty minutes. Alternatively, the vegetables can be cooked under a griller or over an open flame.

Step three: In the meantime, make a white sauce. Warm a little olive oil in a saucepan, add the flour, a little salt and pepper and the freshly ground nutmeg. Stir for two minutes so the ingredients are mixed well. Gradually add the soya milk, stirring constantly so the mixture doesn't become lumpy, until small bubbles appear.

Step four: Place a third of the vegetable-tofu mixture in a large, square or rectangular baking or casserole dish. Cover with some fresh tomato sauce/tomato puree (see earlier recipe for pasta sauce), then a layer of lasagne sheets, then a third of the white sauce. Repeat layers. Top with soya cheese slices.

Step five: Cover with foil (shiny side down) and bake for thirty minutes. Remove the foil and bake for another ten minutes. Serve with fresh green or mixed salad.